Genius! Marketing

Stephen L. Eckert

ISBN 978-0-692-11755-2

DEDICATION

Dedicated to the many companies and people who helped me develop Genius! Marketing… from clients to vendors to associates to friends. However, most of all, this book is dedicated to the greatest genius I ever met, and a fine marketer as well: Louis Eckert III. Thanks, mom, for not letting him name me Louie the fourth.

And to you, dear reader: May All Your Marketing Be Genius!

SLEckert

CONTENTS

ACKNOWLEDGMENTS

Thanks to Michelle and Patty, for this book wouldn't have been finished without your encouragement and persistence.

Thanks to Andy, Fred, Karen, Dave, Mark, Kirk, Alan, Jeff, Jim, Joe, Dan, Joyce, Tracie, Matt, Sarah, Bill, Jenny and especially Mary, Gretchen, and Max. You contributed to this book by choice or not.

1
SO YOU WANT TO BE A MARKETING GENIUS

What is Genius?
If you ask someone this question, you'll get a variety of answers.
"Really smart"
"Brainiac"
"Me!"

You'll also probably get an example such as "Einstein". When we think of "genius" that is what comes to mind. Someone or something that is beyond us due to superior intelligence or ability.

Of course, the word "genius" can be applied to a singular talent as well. A baseball player can be a "genius with the glove". An artist can be a "genius with light and shadow".

If you google this question, you get this result: (at least this is the result I received):

gen·ius
/ˈjēnyəs/ ◀)

noun

1. exceptional intellectual or creative power or other natural ability.
   "she was a teacher of genius"
   synonyms: brilliance, intelligence, intellect, ability, cleverness, brains, erudition, wisdom, fine mind; More

2. a person who is exceptionally intelligent or creative, either generally or in some particular respect.
   "one of the great musical geniuses of the 20th century"
   synonyms: brilliant person, gifted person, mastermind, Einstein, intellectual, great intellect, brain, mind; More

adjective informal

1. very clever or ingenious.
   "a genius marketing ploy"

Really? The first definition under adjective is "a genius marketing ploy"?!?!?! That's pretty cool. However, the connotation of "ploy" is rather editorial. And maybe a bit cynical. We'll discuss that in more depth a bit later.

The definition of genius includes these words: "exceptional", "intelligent", "creative".

Can your marketing be those things? Can your marketing be exceptional, intelligent and creative? Absolutely… but how do you get there?

Getting to Genius

When talking to people interested in marketing their company, product or service better, often there is a focus on ideas, specific tactics or unrealistic expectations. Let's take a look at each:

1. Ideas: A Dime a Dozen

    You may have heard this euphemism. In fact, it is a cliché. Ideas are a dime a dozen. Yet, most companies focus on ideas when thinking about marketing. The idea for a great tagline. The idea for a killer ad. The idea for a promotion that will drive lots of sales.

    I'll give you a real-life example. A small retailer opened a new store. It was along a traveled road in a growing part of the community. It should have been easy to promote the new site. The company's team working on the launch decided they needed to have a promotion for the new location. One of the managers said he asked his wife what she thought. After all, she was in the target demographic which was the target market. Her idea was to give away an expensive, brand name accessory item to anyone who came to the grand opening/first weeks of business. It was agreed that was a great idea. Genius, even.

    Hundreds of the item were purchased. The doors were opened with expectancy. And nothing…

    A few people came to the opening event. Mostly loyal customers from other locations. Few sales were made, a few of the accessory giveaway items were distributed.

    A year later, still not much traffic, few sales, and looking like the location choice was a mistake. But what about our great giveaway idea?!?

    The idea isn't genius. It might be a great idea, but without action, it is just an idea. And ideas are… you know. The problem was there was very little promotion of the giveaway idea. No one knew to come get their giveaway. Some who did come weren't all that interested in the giveaway. Most in the target demographic could easily purchase the item, should they want one. (There were other problems, too. Some problems are beyond marketing.) So a great idea that failed to deliver.

2. Specific Tactic: I Need a…

    Many conversations I have with companies considering doing some marketing revolve around tactical elements of marketing communications. Or more simply, tactics. Tactics are the specific actionable element of marketing: direct mail, advertising, email, etc.

    Companies are often caught up by a specific tactic. For instance, they decide that the latest thing must be their thing. Or they will see a competitor doing something and determine they must implement that tactic as well. Getting fixated on a tactic can be very dangerous.

    Take Social Media as an example. Since Facebook started to attract millions of users, companies have been mesmerized by Social Media. The appeal is significant. First of all, it is "free". Second, anyone can do Social Media. Best of all, there is no barrier to entry. Meaning it is easy to get started: consider the barrier to entry for social media versus the barrier to entry for sending direct mail.

    To send a direct mail piece, you must:

    a. Determine content of direct mail.
    b. Find a mailing list of people or companies that might be interested.
    c. Print the mailer (and possibly) insert into envelope.
    d. Apply postage.
    e. Send mailer.

    That's a lot of work.

    Compare that with Social Media:

    a. Sign up for an account.
    b. Upload your logo.
    c. Presto! You're using Social Media for your business. Endless numbers of people can now see your page, profile or posts. :-\

    Here's a real-life example that isn't about Social Media (because you can take about 30 seconds to find a company on Facebook that has two posts and one photo…from 2010 – maybe it's your own). This example is about an earlier marketing "gold rush". Back in the days of Internet 1.0, the owner of a distribution company caught the vision of Internet 2.0. Unfortunately, it wasn't invented yet. He spent tens of thousands of dollars developing a website that took orders and promised immediate (via FedEx) delivery of large industrial equipment. The site worked because he made it work. It even had "videos" (this is in the day of modems, mind you), or rather multi-image sequences to show product features. Pretty cool.

Too bad it was a total failure. In retrospect, Amazon took ten more years to convince people to buy a book online… why did an industrial specialty distributor think contractors would buy his products that way? He thought that because he became so infatuated with the tactic of marketing via the web that he forgot one critical fact: his customers weren't ready to buy that way. It turned out he was about 15 years ahead of the curve. I'd call that bleeding edge. It significantly impacted his company's profitability. His focus got off the real goal: selling product and onto a marketing tactic.

Whatever the specific tactic is, it is a real problem for a single tactic to be the focus of your marketing.

3.   Unrealistic Expectations: A Million for a Buck

Another mistake companies make is having unrealistic expectations for their marketing. I call this the "Silver Bullet" mentality. Every company is looking for that silver bullet, the one marketing element, tactic or strategy that will work. Not only that will work but will work fast, continue to work and will not cost more than a dollar while making them a million sales. A million for a buck.

An example: a business-to-business professional services company "got in early" on digital marketing. Back when the whole category was called "Adwords". They placed relatively inexpensive ads on Google's advertising platform and received good leads via their pay-per-click advertising. Fast forward three years. Their monthly cost had quadrupled for the same ads/keywords/clicks. Leads still came in, but fewer, and at a higher cost. What happened to their silver bullet? Competition. More companies discovered Adwords and the digital advertising platforms. Salespeople were out calling; agencies were springing up selling "digital ads"; everyone had heard about the silver bullet. The moral is that even when something works, it can't be the only marketing tactic. Relish great response to an ad, but don't assume it is the norm. Celebrate the direct mail piece that gets a 15% response rate, but don't stop spending marketing resources on an integrated marketing mix.

These three may seem like ridiculous examples, and each is hyperbole. I exaggerate to make the point: marketing is not a magic wand or a silver bullet. There is no idea, tactic or potion that instantly and forever makes sales happen. It just doesn't exist. (Though people keep trying to find it!)

Sadly, not even this book is the one answer, although the attempt is to guide you to the one answer.

So What?

Defining these traps that companies fall into is critical. We must re-frame marketing if we want to be good at it. If we're going to become marketing geniuses we must do hard work. While I lay out these three maladies in a way that seems extreme, it is often the thinking behind the conversation about marketing. Rational, intelligent, successful professionals and business owners speak about marketing ideas but lurking behind the statements and questions are these three fallacies. (Warning: all of the following are real examples heard in business meetings. You may recognize them from your own conversations!)

"I just want you to tell me what will work for my business."

"What's the one thing I should do to market my company?"

"I don't have a big budget, we need to be very surgical in what we do."

"Our industry is unique. We need to do (specific tactic here) to make it in this business."

"We have to attend this show. It is the place to be for our industry."

"I've spent lots of money on marketing (or specific tactic here), and it doesn't work."

"We tried (specific tactic or idea here), and we didn't get anything out of it."

"This is the way to reach millennials. This will get us a younger customer."

"I saw this done by XYZ and they have a ton of sales."

"If we just do this, we will be in front of all of our prospects."

All of these statements within a more extensive discussion of marketing strategy may be helpful. However, often these statements are the "whole" conversation, and once the idea, tactic or expectation is decided or takes hold, it's game over. The tactic has become the plan, the whole plan and nothing but the plan. Marketing failure is coming… it's just a matter of time.

It seems like the right time to introduce the Genius Marketing motto. It also happens to be a quote from a verified genius: Thomas Edison. In case you've forgotten your school lessons, Edison invented the lightbulb. And the phonograph. And the motion picture camera. And the stock ticker. And a working power station. And just for kicks, an electric car battery more than a century before Elon musked.

Here's what Edison said about genius:

Genius is
1%
inspiration
and
99%
perspiration

Translation: it's not the idea. It's the work to make the idea work.

Unfortunately, there are many genuine reasons that companies and their owners and managers fall for these fallacies of marketing. So we can avoid, the idea, the tactic and the bullet, let's look at how the fall can happen.

1. Business…or rather Busyness

    Everyone is busy. With limited time and a focus on other job and life responsibilities, it narrows the field of focus. We can only take in so much information. We are exposed to only some of the possibilities for marketing. There is no way a CEO, CFO, Director, Market Manager, Owner or any other person in business can know how to market.

    However, we do have some field of focus; we do take in some information; we are exposed to some marketing. This reality, in conjunction with our second point, can be disastrous.

2. Everyone is a Marketer

    Everyone believes they are a marketer. That was the discussion when a friend of mine, Andy Reeher, used this analogy to illustrate the problem: No one would consider themselves an accountant because they balance a checkbook (or now more relatable: because they use a financial app). However, everyone believes they are a marketer because they have consumed marketing. That's because we all have opinions about marketing. Just get on the internet the day after the Super Bowl (or on social media during the game).

    So people who have limited time, access and expertise in marketing, however, they have consumed marketing, and believe they know how to market. The combination of these leads to a simple result: they become convinced they have the right idea, tactic or expectation for their marketing. None of this comes from data, but they are satisfied. Alas, they will be disappointed 99% of the time. However, not before they encounter our third reason for believing the marketing fallacies.

3. Salespeople

    Salespeople are awesome. An associate, Fred Perrotta, titled his book, "Nothing Happens Until a Sale is Made". True words. Props to all who sell. That said (and I mean it!), there is a problem when busy owners, managers, and executives buy marketing. Salespeople selling an idea, tactic (or even an expectation) can reinforce the fallacies of marketing.

    For a radio salesperson, the reach and portability of radio mean it is the right fit for your company.

    A printer will show you statistics on how consumers still use and prefer printed sales sheets or flyers to learn about offers and sales.

    The digital agency will have slide after slide (or infographics) of data showing that it's all about the internet (or the mobile display ad network).

Are they lying? Of course not. However, it is a pattern that leads to marketing failure. Or at least limited results. The formula:

$$\text{A Salesperson} + \text{Limited Access to Options} = \text{Belief in Our Ideas}$$

The Salesperson's limited offering in conjunction with the limited access and focus of the buyer, multiplied by the pre-conceived belief in one idea, tactic or expectation, compounded by the desire to find the one silver bullet of marketing equals…

Well, you can imagine the result. The company pursues a slice of the marketing pie and misses out on the entire dessert tray. Maybe it will work. I hope so. (You know what they say about hope…it's not a plan.)

So if these are the fallacies, what is the truth about marketing?

Marketing Truth

There are things you can count on when marketing. It is not a complete gambit or ploy. One thing you can count on: you need to do it.

Without marketing (and the related/integrated sales effort), nothing happens, just as Fred said in his book. Beyond this fact, there are a few principles to avoid the fallacies and become a genius marketer.

1. Everything is a Test

    When considering any idea, tactic or expectation, re-frame marketing not primarily as a guarantee of results, but as a test. In doing so, we can begin to break through the emotion and appeal of an idea and look at the variables involved in making the idea or tactic a success. Plus the bonus of setting realistic expectations for results.

2. The River moves fast, but the ocean is deep.

    The latest thing is always tempting, but in marketing, it is often better to be somewhat behind "the bleeding edge" to gain an understanding of what to expect from an idea or tactic and what best practices are developing for the tactic.

    So while we may want to jump in the river which is moving fast, there are very few marketing opportunities which are a "must have", "right now" or "all is lost", opportunity. Better to be in the ocean with its depth and breadth. The ocean still makes an impact with its waves but has much more significant reserves than the river.

On to Genius: The One Thing You Need

The purpose of this book is to show you how to make your company a genius marketing company. Certainly, ideas, tactics and even expectations will be a part of Genius Marketing. However, none of these will drive the marketing. That will be reserved for the one thing that a company must do to be genius. The one thing is: developing a marketing process.

Part strategy, part action or implementation plan, the marketing process is what makes genius marketing happen. It is the arbiter of what ideas are worth pursuing, it evaluates and maximizes tactics, and it is the framework for reasonable, achievable and trackable expectations.

Small businesses, and the people within them, prioritize marketing this way:
1.   Idea
2.   Implementation
3.   Process

And typically there would only be two numbers on the list or, number three is "Results". The boss or owner has an idea, gets someone to implement it, and that's it. Maybe they track results for the idea, but most times, not. Results are just an impression of how things went with the idea.

For a genius marketing company, the process must become the priority. A process with ideas and implementation and results.

Yes, the results are subject to the process, too. Why? Because we want repeatable results. So we see this idea and implementation and a test. We see it as a part of a bigger process – the sales and marketing process. So while we want ideas, we also want to implement them well. We want good results, and we want this idea to be part of something bigger that consistently delivers leads, opportunities, prospects, and ultimately, sales.

No, the marketing process is not that sexy. It's not the most fun. It isn't what people think of when asked about marketing. However, it is the one thing that a company must do to market well. It is the heart and soul of Genius Marketing!

CHAPTER 1
TAKEAWAYS

1. Marketing isn't easy. It's work. Part art/part science.

2. Don't fall for the fallacy of a single idea or particular tactic.

3. No single marketing anything results in a million sales.

4. Marketing is always a test; take the long view. Even when you need immediate sales.

5. Build a marketing process. A process that is an ongoing lead generator for your organization.

2
ASSESSMENT: START AT THE BEGINNING

"Begin at the beginning," the King said, gravely, "and go on till you come to the end; then stop." – Alice in Wonderland

It may be overstating it to say that Marketing as a discipline is a wonderland. Still, there are, as with any field of study, many complexities and intricacies. Especially with the way marketing is always evolving with technology, personalization, data diving, and so much more. That's why it is so important to start at the beginning in order to have marketing success.

As discussed in the first chapter, when it comes to marketing, it starts with the idea. So at the end of this chapter, please take time to write down all of your marketing ideas. The things that you'd like to do to market your business. The things that you think your business needs. Even the things that you hope will bring you the 'million sales for one dollar' mentioned earlier.

Write down every idea that brought you to the place where you thought "I need a book on marketing…"

Write down the thing that comes to mind when told your company needs more sales.

Write down the things you see other companies doing that you think would be great for your company… or that you read about in INC or Entrepreneur or your favorite marketing blog.

Write down every marketing idea you can. At the end of this chapter is space to do this exercise.

Moving On

Once you have your ideas noted, set them aside. Yes, we'll come back to them… but for now, leave them be.

Now let's go back to the beginning of your company. Not historically (necessarily) but to the real genius idea of what you do and why people buy from you.

It's time to get to work on your marketing.

Start with Goal Setting

When I work with clients in person, I always start with two questions:
What is your goal for the process?

What is the goal of your marketing?

These are two different questions. In this case (not a live consulting situation), the first question, it is better asked… what do you want to get out of this book?

This is important. You may have picked up the book because you want to get an idea or two. Most of the people I talk to answer the question one (or multiple) of these:

1. I need to know how much money to spend on marketing.
2. I am spending money on marketing, but I don't know how well it's working.
3. I have a new product or brand, and I'm not sure how to market it.
4. I need to learn how to use social media.
5. I have a website, and I run some ads, but I know I could get more out of marketing/advertising.
6. I need a plan.

These reasons may or may not sync with the answers to the next question: What are your goals for your marketing? One response to this question for every organization should be: TO INCREASE SALES. There are many possible goals for marketing, but ultimately the purpose of marketing is to help get more sales and build top line revenue.

At the end of this chapter in the exercises, do your best to note two, three, four goals for the process and your marketing. What you hope to get out of this book.

In the Beginning…

Now let's work on a description of your company.

What do you do? How do you do it? Here are a couple of examples:

XYZ Corp is:
- A successful, viable entity that has dozens of customers and serves a metro region.
- It is looking to expand sales to existing customers and find new business.
- For existing customers, it wants to add sales in the area of services related to the product.
- It is unclear regarding the new business - it may ramp up production and continue with its primary product; or it may branch out into a new product line.
- Need to define products/services - they have evolved in response to customer requests rather than strategically
- Have tried "typical" marketing promotions such as discounts, grouping products into packages and providing free shipping
- Not afraid to be innovative, but success is based on the people who champion new ideas

ABC LLC is:
- Very young, started under two years ago.
- Had initial growth based on existing relationships from previous business and employment situations.
- Has too much of its revenue coming from a few sources; needs to expand its customer base.
- Has not advertised or promoted itself beyond a web presence.
- Is in a highly competitive market and struggles with pricing to value because of competition.
- Needs to grow to reach revenue that opens up opportunities for scale.
- Gets things done through the hard work of a handful of faithful staff who love the company and have been with it from the start

What is your situation? It is sometimes hard to put to paper (or pixels), but it is difficult to move forward with marketing without having a realistic view of the situation. Use the questions below to help you assess your situation. If need be, talk to people you trust who don't have a vested interest in your company… that means people who aren't employees, customers or suppliers (they all have an investment interest in one way or another). Best way to do this is to write out your situation and then show it to other business owners or professionals who are in similar market situations, but not in your direct industry or your competition.

Situation Questions (see end of chapter for form version):
1. Give a brief overview of the purpose of your company… what do you do?

2. What is your product or service?

3. How big are you? How old?

4. How do you provide this service/product?

5. What is the biggest challenge to fulfilling your mission? Or to your promise to customers?

6. What is the best thing this company does?

7. If you could add one more capability to your team, what would it be?

8. What is your market like? How much competition? What is your reputation in the market?

9. If you had to use three words to describe your company as perceived by your customers, what would they be? (three words, not a phrase, i.e. trustworthy, responsive, quality or fast, expensive, exclusive)

This exercise may be easy, or it may be very difficult. Take your time in working through it. Sometimes, I ask clients to think about it this way… if you were writing a letter to a friend you hadn't spoken with for a few years, but you trusted very deeply, how would you describe your situation?

Write that person a letter (for exercise purposes only - you don't have to send it) describing your situation, your company. Explain where you are and where you want to go. It may sound like an odd exercise, but can actually be very helpful… when you confess to a friend you trust in a long conversation (or letter) you will tend to get past your near-term perceptions and begin to uncover the reality of your situation. Give it a try. And feel free to send the letter if you like.

Check Your Perceptions
After you answer the questions (or write the letter), review it with others in your company. Explain you are working on some planning and want to get their input on the current situation. Realize they may have an agenda, and they certainly have a perspective based on their professional role/expertise, and their relationship with you and your organization.

Once you think you have a good grasp on the internal view, work on finding someone outside the company (and its sphere of influence as stated above) to review the situation. If you can find someone who cares about you, and your company, but not their stake in it, you will get good solid opinions about the state of your business situation.

You will also get ideas. Very few people are capable of having a conversation such as we're describing without giving their opinion. Be polite, accept the ideas without judgment, add them to the list of ideas made earlier... and move on to the next step.

Marketing Inventory

The next assessment step is to conduct an audit of your marketing elements. That's a fancy way of saying write down what marketing your company is doing now. Be as complete as possible, including promotions (such as contests and sales/discounts), marketing communications (such as advertising), sales support or collateral materials (such as product sheets), branded items (such as letterhead, signage, advertising specialties), online presence, events, and so on...

Typically, the list might look like this:
- Website
- email newsletter
- sales sheets
- Linkedin
- giveaway items - pens, caps, calendars
- direct mail
- annual golf outing
- summer sale
- regional trade show
- networking group/chamber

This list will be referenced later when we are building the tactical and content plans.

Profiling Your Targets

The next step in our assessment process is profiling. When considering your marketing the first person to think about is the prospect. The prospect is the goal of your marketing. Along with customers, to whom you market to reinforce their good buying decision, and to cross-sell, up-sell and provide renewal/replacement sales. Take the time to profile your best customers. Unless the products and services of your organization are about to change drastically, your customer profile is the best way to build a prospect profile.

Start with sales records... to whom are current sales made? As you build your first prospect profile think about who is buying and why they are buying. Work through the list below to develop a profile.

Cloning Your Customers

Data companies can take your customer list and "clone" it. Add prospects that "look like" your current customers to your database. Base this cloning on organizational data points like size, the number of employees, annual sales, geography, industry/SIC code and contact data points like title, job function and more. There is nothing wrong with using a data service to get more leads for your outbound marketing and direct selling efforts.

That said, it is still valuable to understand more than data points about your customers. Data mining is important, but understanding why people and organizations buy is essential as well. Especially in small to mid-size companies, people often are the reason for the sale. This is not to diminish the role of people at the large enterprise level, but suffice it to say, the smaller the company, the more the people matter.

An example:
I was assessing a new client's business. A contractor which designed and built large, green structures such as churches, office buildings, retail, etc. When we began profiling customers (who bought and why), the needed marketing strategy was obvious.

Me: "How did you meet the office complex customer?"
Client: "I met him at my sportsman's club, we served together on a committee."
Me: "How did you get the church campus project?"
Client: "One of the administrators at the church was working on a rehab project at my sportsman's club. She and I ended up on the crew that rebuilt a small footbridge over a fishing stream."
Me: "From where did the retail shop project come?"
Client: "Oh I've known the Smiths forever, they're both longtime members of the sportsman's club."

And on it went. Every major project came from a personal interaction at the club. Finally, I said his partner should find a club to join. He responded his partner had just joined a biking club. I probably could have left at that point. Clearly, for their size company, and the engaging service-minded people they are, just living and sharing life with people gained them a lot of business.

There were other marketing issues, as always, and I was able to help them open other prospecting channels. Still, their bread and butter on marketing and sales were their people. So as you work through the following list (and feel free to do more than one - products and services can have more than one profile of customer) try to understand why people buy. Look for common reasons. Attributes of them (or you and your organization) that link them together. That will be critical as we move forward with your marketing plan.

Profile of a typical customer
Company
    Location (geography)
    Size employees
    Units or locations

SIC/Type/Industry
Revenue
Sales
Age
Growth
Stage of company evolution
Organizational/Leadership structure
Place in supply chain
Contact
Title
Role in company
Work style
Where do they live
Age
How Found
Why did they buy
What about your organization do they like
Commitment level to your organization
Interests beyond work

Other Variables: unique attributes of the customer or their relationship to your company

Once you begin to understand who your best customers are, take another look through the data (hard data or anecdotal information you or your team "know") to pick out variables of commonality. It could be demographic information (all our best customers are in Mayberry Township), or it could be other variables that may indicate why they buy (our best contacts are all managers not at the home office of the company who we support because they have limited staff). In the Genius Marketing consulting practice we are open to working with any company, but our best customers – the ones that we provide the most value and frankly, enjoy working with the most – all have a common variable: we work directly with the owner/top manager/CEO, and the company is not large enough or established enough to have a set of VPs of Marketing, Sales, and Business Development. We end up working directly for the CEO in the role of "Virtual VP of Marketing". This key variable cuts across industry and other demographic information… it is the "intangible" on which we've been able to identify and focus our effort. So, take the time to figure out the key variable of your best customers.

Key Variables of our customers are:
Company

Individual

Finally, at least for this profiling exercise set, write out detailed profiles of your target markets. Create a narrative - at least a short paragraph that describes in a way that you can see the "person".

An example:

For one client we started to look at their customers (data-driven analysis) and found that their best customers were older. The owner had mentioned "getting younger" as a goal of Marketing and Human Resources. This financial services company was built on relationships with customers who over time had aged. Many relationship-driven/trusted-advisor businesses are like this – whether doctor, lawyer, insurance or investments, it is common for trusted advisors to have customers of relatively the same age as the provider. One of the reasons bringing more (younger) professionals into the company was a priority. The data confirmed what she "knew", the overall average age of the business's customers was in their mid-fifties. So the team brainstormed specifically what some profile prospects would "look like".

Jessica

Jessica is a young, professional woman living or working in the (zip codes) area. She is 25 - 34 and a college graduate. She is a new homeowner or is looking to find a first home. Her income may range from $50,000 and up. She is not married, but may be in a relationship. She is independent, smart and makes decisions based on data, with just a touch of intuition and "right feel".

William

William is approaching middle age - 35 - 40. He lives or works in the (zip codes) area. He may be married, and has children. He is a manager, whether retail, industrial or professional. He is starting to consider the future for himself and his family. He is smart in his field but is aware he is not an expert in all areas and appreciates input on financial matters. His income is $60,000 and up.

Brian and Tracy

A committed married couple with children, they are starting to see the fruits of their labor. They may or may not both work, but their income is sufficient to fund their family's lifestyle. They are in their forties with school-aged children, and they realize college is on the horizon. They typically make financial decisions together, although they have different tolerances for risk. Their income is $80,000 and up.

If we were considering marketing to these target markets, the benefit of such a profile is clear: the creative team, sales people and customer service staff can "see" who we are targeting. It makes choosing the right product offering and developing the messaging for each profile easier. Data can help us round out the target market. For example, answering questions such as how big is our target market? (How many people exist in each of these profile categories in our target geography?)

Two caveats:

We will sell to anyone (mostly). Although we target specifically, I often hear that "everyone is our target customer". That is true if you are selling air or water. However, even in those products, there are limiting factors which help us define our market better. We profile to limit the focus of our marketing, but we never limit the availability of our product or service. The danger in saying "we sell to everyone" or more illustratively put "everyone wants our product" – we may fall prey to marketing too widely. Unless we have unlimited time, money and energy, our marketing to "everyone" will fail.

Conversely, if we tighten our focus, we usually open up more opportunity. It helps us more clearly communicate our value proposition and buying rationale. It even helps us communicate with suppliers who are trying to help us. Remember back in chapter one where we talked about falling in love with a salesperson's offering? They offered, we went for it? When we explicitly explain our target market/persona, our advertising partners may have different recommendations to best reach our audience.

There is an essential profile missing. Did you notice its absence? There is no profile representing the current customers of the example company. In the example above, I made it clear that we wanted to profile our existing customers. There may be more of the current profile to whom we can sell. Also, we always want to reinforce to existing customers that they are of great import and we are not abandoning them for a new (in this case, younger) customer. All of our external marketing efforts may focus on our new target markets. Still, we need to maintain appropriate communication with our existing customers as part of a retention or cross- or up-sell strategy.

Good Data in...
The adage "garbage in, garbage out" also works in the positive: Taking the time to profile customers and unpack the attributes that are the reasons people buy provides the good data that will lead to an excellent marketing plan and process.

CHAPTER 2
EXERCISES

1. Write down your marketing ideas.

    _____
    _____
    _____
    _____
    _____
    _____
    _____
    _____
    _____
    _____
    _____
    _____
    _____
    _____
    _____
    _____
    _____
    _____
    _____
    _____
    _____

    Set these ideas aside (mentally)… for now.

2. What is your goal(s) for the process? What do you want to get out of the book?

    _____
    _____
    _____
    _____
    _____
    _____

3. What is the goal for your marketing?

    _____
    _____
    _____
    _____
    _____
    _____

4. Current Marketing
    Specials/Promotions

    _____
    _____
    _____

    Marketing Communications and Advertising

    _____
    _____
    _____

    Sales Support/Collateral

    _____
    _____
    _____

    Branded Items

    _____
    _____
    _____

    Outbound Marketing (direct mail, email, phone calls, etc.)

    _____
    _____
    _____

    Online and Digital

    _____
    _____
    _____

    Events

    _____
    _____
    _____

    Networking

    _____
    _____
    _____

    Other

    _____
    _____
    _____

5. Profiling Your Customers

Company
    Location   _____
    Size/employees   _____
    Units or locations   _____
    SIC/Type/Industry   _____
    Revenue   _____
    Sales   _____
    Age   _____
    Growth   _____
    State of company   _____
    Leadership structure _____
    Place in supply chain _____

Contact
    Title   _____
    Role in company   _____
    Work style   _____
    Where do they live   _____
    Age   _____
    How found   _____
    Why did they buy   _____
    Like about your co.   _____
    Commitment level   _____
    Other interests   _____

6. Other Variables: unique attributes of the customer or their relationship to your company

_____
_____
_____

7. Commonality: what are the ways our customers are alike that are a reason they buy from us?

_____
_____
_____

8. Customer/Prospect Profile 1:

    _____

    _____

    _____

9. Customer/Prospect Profile 2:

    _____

    _____

    _____

10. Customer/Prospect Profile 3:

    _____

    _____

    _____

11. Customer/Prospect Profile 4:

    _____

    _____

    _____

Take time to work through these questions and begin to build a set of good data that can be used as the foundation for an effective marketing process.

3
HOW SALES ARE MADE

"I don't care if he stands on his head in the batter's box... if he can hit." –
attributed to Connie Mack, Hall of Fame Manager.

You may have heard the saying that "It's not the people, it's the process." Marketing is a process. Supporting the sales effort is a process. Unfortunately, most small businesses' marketing is done by people with little or no process. People (or a person) is the process. A typical example (that I hope you don't recognize):

With the rise of email marketing platforms (Constant Contact, MailChimp, iContact, etc.), many companies saw an easy way to contact customers and prospects. It is an excellent communications channel (even though many people have tired of receiving countless promotional emails). Owners and managers saw the low cost compared to other marketing channels, the ease of using the platforms, and (probably) competitors running email campaigns.

Commonly, someone in the office was assigned to investigate email providers and set up an email newsletter or promotional/product offer emails. Let's call him Bob. The boss gave Bob (let's call her Sue) the first subjects for the email: a new product, a current promotion or discount, or information about the company. Bob did the assigned work and began sending emails.

However, Sue and Bob didn't create a process for email as an ongoing marketing element within a marketing plan. Bob developed the layouts and content, and Sue approved them. It worked well. At least for a while.

Typically, such an effort starts to lose steam very quickly. Sue or Bob may get busy with other tasks. Bob may run out of ideas for content and Sue isn't able to take the time from running the business to organize or create new content. Others in the organization haven't been made aware of the email effort (even though they may receive the emails), and are not engaged in providing ideas or content. Results may not be as expected and disappoint. The influence of the emails isn't understood or coordinated with other marketing and sales initiatives. There is no urgency or accountability to keep the "process" moving.

A monthly email becomes quarterly, then periodic. Then never. True story.

Another scenario is that Sue or Bob change positions in the company, or leave the organization. Since the process was indeed a person, when the person leaves, the process goes with them.

Either way, the result is that because the people are the process, when the people become busy, distracted or leave, there is no one to be the process.

The same is true for a marketing plan. There is a plan, but it doesn't exist on paper. That's why in the profiling section we went through the exercise of writing down all the marketing tactics used within your organization. Those are the ideas being implemented, so we want to capture them as the existing marketing plan.

When a plan is only in the mind of a person, the plan may walk out the door (when the person leaves the company). That is a risk. More realistic is the plan not being implemented because the plan holder's mind, time and energy are focused on other work (not the marketing plan). Marketing will happen when marketing happens.

The marketing plan must be what drives the marketing process. The marketing process is what makes the marketing happen. The process manages the implementation of the plan.

So What is Our Process?

Since the role of marketing is to support the sales effort, we start with the sales process. Even awareness advertising and brand building activities ultimately must have the goal of achieving more sales.

Sometimes marketing has a straightforward connection to how sales happen. In an e-commerce or retail setting, marketing may be the direct cause of a transaction. In other situations, where sales are made through a salesforce, marketing is in the role of creating interest and guiding prospects to the salesforce (or the salesforce to prospects). That is why it is critical for proper marketing to start with how sales happen.

When the two (marketing and sales) become disconnected, it is usually because of the age-old feud. Marketing says that sales are not doing anything with the wonderful leads provided; Sales says that marketing ignores their needs and doesn't get them any leads. Usually, the quality of leads isn't the problem. The problem is that there is no integration of the full sales process. In academics (at least back in the day), "Marketing" represented the entire process of delivering a product to the customer, from identifying the need to making a sale that solved the customer's problem.

Today, in most companies, Sales and Marketing are very separate things. Sales may have a couple of folks who can get a hit when they are standing on their head. Everyone leaves them alone, because "they get it done". Not a problem, until you try to replace them or add another one of them.

Meanwhile, Marketing focuses on creative. Creative campaigns, ads, social media contests, and so on.

And never shall the two meet. Even in small organizations where the owner or a few top managers are responsible for sales coming in AND for managing the marketing, the two disciplines are on separate paths. However, there is only one path, grasshopper. Marketing's sole function is to support sales. Sales' role is an extension of marketing steps – the final steps in the Marketing (capitalized academic "M") process.

Mapping the Process
To understand how marketing can best support sales, we must understand each step in the sales process. Every sale has a process, although it may not be apparent as a series of steps. That's why we must map the process.

Your sales team has a process. It may not be written down, but it is probably understood... maybe. If asked, a salesperson can tell you the process:
"I take the lead and email asking for a meeting. Then I call. If I get the meeting, I work discovery and find out which product would work for their situation. I do a cost estimate/proposal. Then I close the sale."

That's the sales process. In reading that you, no doubt, immediately started thinking of questions you'd ask the salesperson:
What if they don't respond to the email or call?
What if the meeting doesn't get you the information you need?
What if the sale doesn't close?

Those are good questions, and there are more reasonable ones to ask. That's why we want to map our process. So everyone knows the steps. Marketing may have an excellent solution for when the call doesn't get a response. The sales manager or boss probably has an idea of what to do with prospects that don't close. (That sounds more ominous than intended.)

The point is that if we map the steps, we help facilitate a better process, better communication, ways to improve the process, and so on...

How are current sales being made?

Are the variables that are key to sales addressed in the marketing process?

How Much Process?

The sales process is different for every company. It may be very formal, informal or downright serendipitous. We might want to use a more consultative process or very direct selling techniques. It varies and with good reason: every company is different. While processes may look similar, they should be unique to the organization and the situation.

Earlier we read an informal process as related by an unknown salesperson. On the next page is a more formal process. In this process, we see the full range of questions we can include in our mapping process. In fact, each of the steps in this process could have multiple sub-steps. The point is not to map the process to death, but to provide enough detail that the marketing team, salesforce and management know what the process is and how to evaluate success.

Marketing/Sales Process Overview

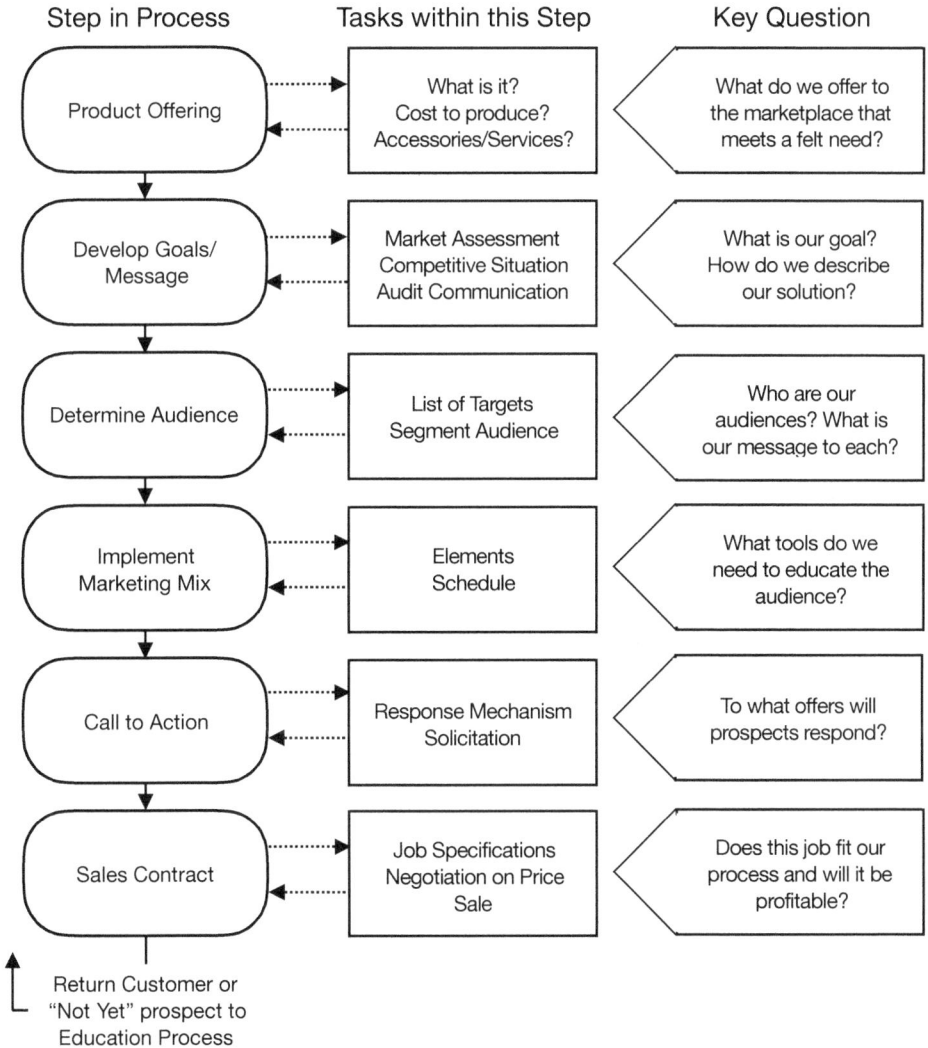

Step in Process	Tasks within this Step	Key Question
Product Offering	What is it? Cost to produce? Accessories/Services?	What do we offer to the marketplace that meets a felt need?
Develop Goals/ Message	Market Assessment Competitive Situation Audit Communication	What is our goal? How do we describe our solution?
Determine Audience	List of Targets Segment Audience	Who are our audiences? What is our message to each?
Implement Marketing Mix	Elements Schedule	What tools do we need to educate the audience?
Call to Action	Response Mechanism Solicitation	To what offers will prospects respond?
Sales Contract	Job Specifications Negotiation on Price Sale	Does this job fit our process and will it be profitable?

Return Customer or
"Not Yet" prospect to
Education Process

I like the flowchart mapping. Sometimes it is vertical, sometimes horizontal. We've found that it helps people grasp the steps more easily. However, You may choose a more narrative approach.

Here is an example of a narrative about the process for an accounting firm:

Our current process is informal. We attend events, give out literature, do some mailing, advertising, but we do not formally follow-up. Prospects must "raise their hand" and then we engage them. Our referral network is the most formal aspect of our process.

When a prospect does self-identify, we set a meeting to understand the business and its issues, and then in a follow-up mailing/email propose a range of work and costs. We then follow up with a phone call to close the business. Typically this closing call is to set up the first meeting to pick up financials. Sometimes the follow-up meeting closes the sale.

Anyone in the organization can understand the process by reading a couple of paragraphs. It is the context by which others in the firm can help improve the process:
- Can we improve our follow-up with a series of emails about the benefits of working with the firm?
- Could we increase "raising hands" by inviting the prospects to a webinar about the importance of sound financial practices or the latest financial regulation?
- Do we set an automatic tickler to check back with non-responders in a week, month or quarter? Could someone else in the organization (not the accountants) make additional follow-up calls?

How Return Sales Are Made
Organizations often under-appreciate their customers. Our marketing should include our customers, and even if we're not looking to create add-on sales, we should be reinforcing the great decision they made by becoming a customer. However, for most companies, the goal is additional sales, a renewal of a contract, an upgrade to a bigger package, a maintenance contract, etc. That's why we also want to map return sales processes.

For our accounting firm, the return process is critical:

Our current process is formal...at least for tax work. All customers receive the quarterly newsletter. Then at year end, an information packet is sent to prepare for the tax work.

Clear and concise. Again, you probably already are seeing ways to improve the process. That's the genius of focusing on the process... when you start to frame marketing this way it provides the context and means to add to and alter the process for the better. Suddenly, your ideas and tactics have a place to reside. You are thinking about applying ideas and tactics to the overall process to improve it.

This is sometimes called "challenging the champion". We'll call whatever we map as the current process the "champion" (it's gotten you this far!). Then as we go through the work of Genius Marketing, we'll start to "attack" the champion and see if we can test (marketing is always a test) a new/better way of some aspect of our marketing process. You can call it "continuous improvement" or A/B testing, but the point is we want to be working on the process to get better results consistently.

Use the templates at the end of this chapter to map your current process for sales and return sales. If you have multiple products or services that you sell through different methods, map each distinctive sales process. An example would be selling a product via a retail distribution chain and selling that same product directly to consumers via the company website.

CHAPTER 3
TAKEAWAYS AND EXERCISES

1. Write out your sales process steps or use the flowchart template on the following page.

Our sales process is

_____

_____

_____

_____

_____

_____

_____

_____

_____

_____

_____

_____

_____

_____

_____

_____

_____

_____

_____

_____

_____

_____

2. Write out your returning sales process steps or use the flowchart template on the following pages.

Our return sales process is

_____

_____

_____

_____

_____

_____

_____

_____

_____

_____

_____

_____

_____

_____

_____

_____

_____

_____

_____

_____

_____

_____

How Sales are Made Flowchart Template

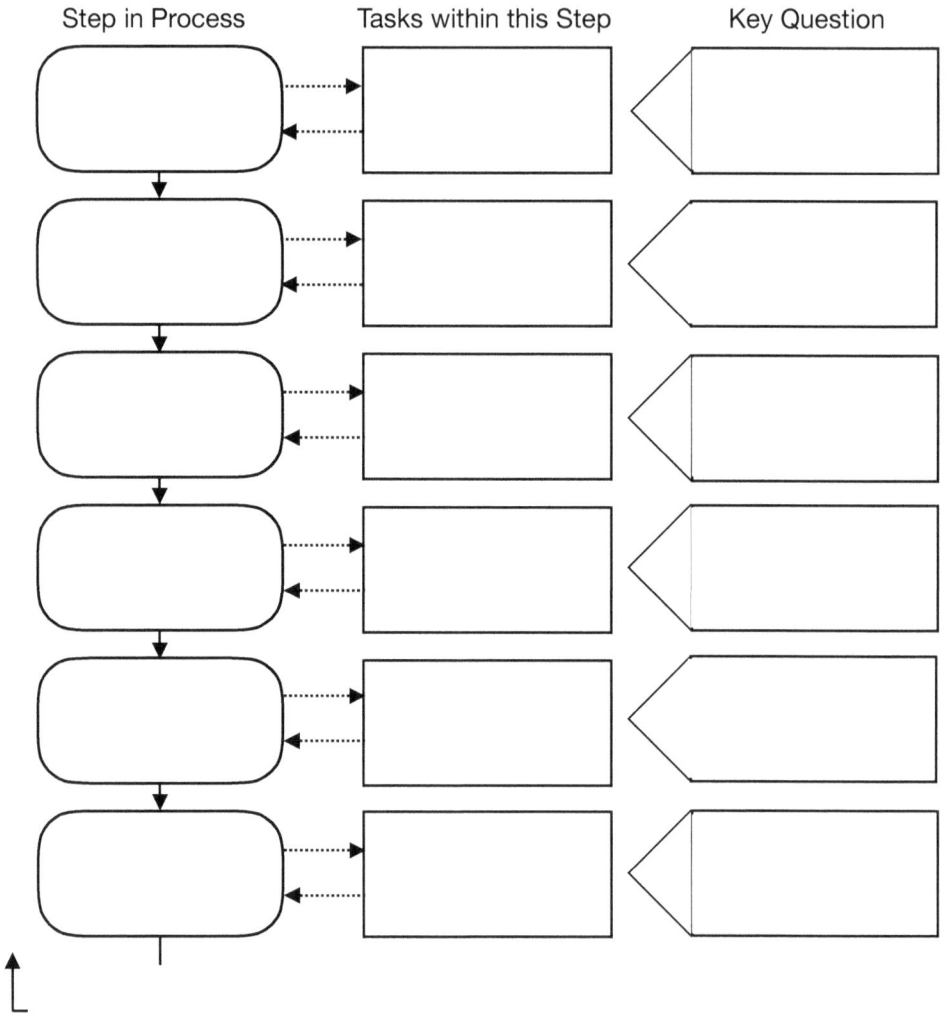

Step in Process	Tasks within this Step	Key Question

How Return Sales are Made Flowchart Template

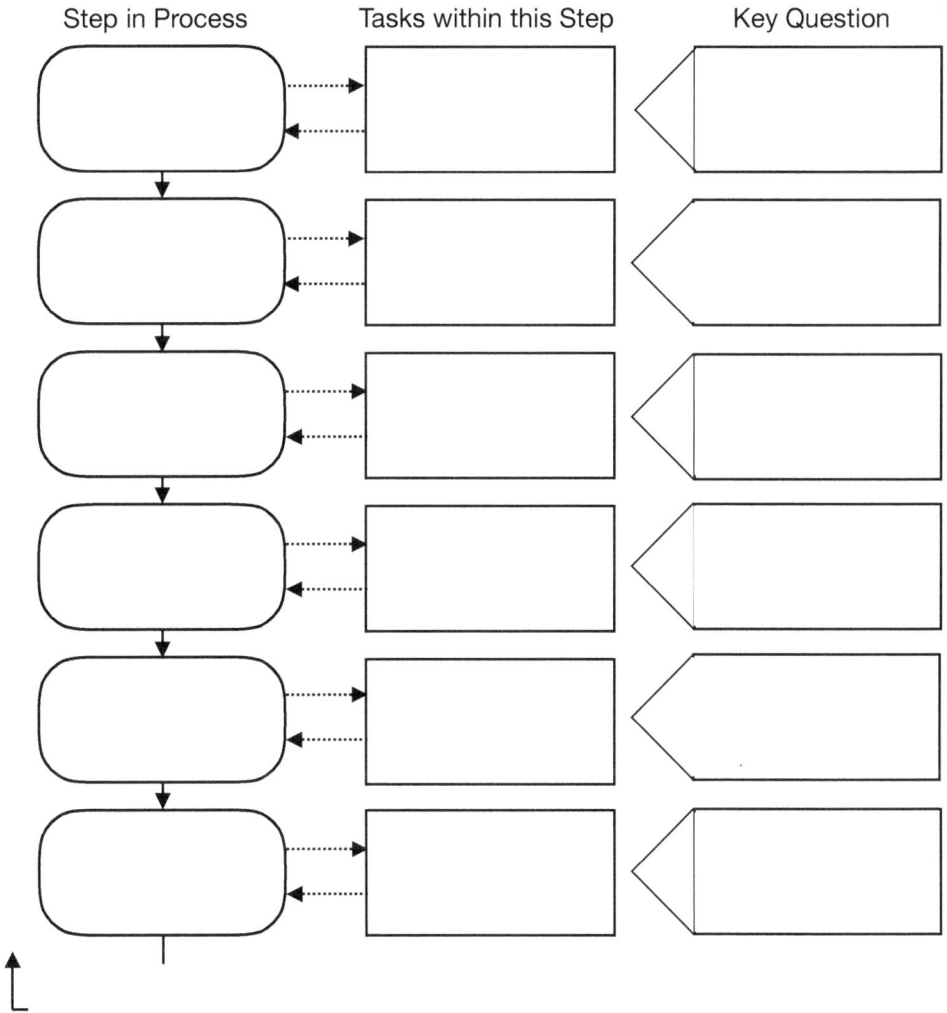

Step in Process	Tasks within this Step	Key Question

4
THE ORGANIZATIONAL BRAND

"To be trusted is a greater compliment than being loved."
– George MacDonald, Scottish Novelist

What is a brand?
When business owners or professionals are asked about their organization's brand, they typically think of logos and graphics, or possibly a tagline. That is because these icons of a brand are powerfully communicated to us as consumers.

Since we all consume so much marketing, the graphics and images used in advertising and other marketing materials become synonymous with "the brand".

Look at the brands that follow. Take a moment to note what immediately comes to mind. Write down your answer describing:
- What visual/image first came to mind?
- What words would you use to describe this brand?
- Of the thoughts you note, which is the most important one word or phrase you would use to describe this brand if you were marketing or selling it?

Mercedes Benz _____
_____
_____

McDonald's _____
_____
_____

Pittsburgh Steelers _____
_____
_____

How did you answer? For Mercedes did you say "Quality"? "Status symbol?" "Overpriced?"

For McDonald's? "Fast?" "Consistent?" "Yuck?"

Steelers? "Tough?" "Winners?" "Whiners?"

Your ability to quickly answer these questions reveals that you understand brands. You may have instantly "seen" the Mercedes three-line crest/logo, the "golden arches" or the black and gold jersey or hypocycloids that make up the Steelers logo. Beyond those visuals/images, the fact that you could write down ideas that those names connote shows that the business activities of the brands have impacted your thinking. Perhaps the product (watching a Steelers game or riding in a Benz) shaped your thinking, perhaps the company's advertising or messaging guided your answer ("I'm Lovin' it"). Maybe others' perceptions impacted your view (online reviews, complaints from a friend, etc.).

The answers I noted show a bit of how perspective matters in how one views a brand. If you drive a Mercedes and I drive a Ford, we may have very different views. If you have kids that eat when you take them to family night at McDonald's your view will be very different from a family with dietary issues and allergies.

Guess what? I'm from Pittsburgh… so my answers might differ greatly from you on the Steelers. Especially if you are from Baltimore, Cincinnati, or Cleveland.

The reason I included "consistent" in the McDonald's brand attributes list is that there was a time when this was one of the biggest brand attributes of McDonald's. For many years, a McDonald's sign on a long family drive meant consistency: a restaurant layout that the family recognized, a burger and fries the kids would eat (because it was exactly the same as the one 200 miles down the road) and clean bathrooms. Yes, really, clean bathrooms. (Brands change over time.)

A friend of mine lives in Cleveland. For years, he complained about how dirty, mean, and awful the Steelers were. Based on facts…so called. An occasional bad hit, a penalty that went against the Steelers, an injury that was attributed to a "dirty player".

I, as a faithful Pittsburgher, could list brand attributes of the Steelers for days and not come up with "dirty" or "mean" on my list. My list would focus on the stability of the organization and ownership, the culture of winning, the skill of the defense, and so on…

So, is brand just in the eye of the beholder? Is our brand only valuable because the customer applies value? Yes and no. There is no way to completely overcome a potential customer's perspective (or prejudice) about our brand.

However, the brand is not beholden to the viewer. The brand is the collection of attributes of an organization. Perspective doesn't change this. It may assign differing values to the attributes, but the attributes are definitions or descriptors of what the organization embodies.

Let's get back to my Cleveland friend. We once had a rational, rather than emotional, discussion about the Steelers and Browns (once). When talking more about the teams and owners and organizations, he admitted the attributes of toughness and stability and winning (rather than "whining") of the Steelers. Those attributes go beyond perspective. He even admitted that he wished the Browns had some of the attributes of the Steelers. That's a key factor of branding… it must communicate real and true attributes that anyone (almost) will acknowledge.

In the same way, the attributes of your organization are true, and not dependent on the perspective of the customer. Their experience and position affect their view, but not the brand.

That's why it's important to build a "real" brand. Work on building an organization that is focused on and committed to things that matter to you (assuming you are a manager or owner of the business), to key stakeholders like partners, shareholders and staff, and to potential customers. It is also why I dislike the idea of "creating a brand". A brand isn't created out of the thin air. It is built and communicated. The communication of the brand can (should) be creative, but the creative isn't the brand. So set aside your thoughts on logo and tagline for a minute and focus on defining your organization's brand.

Start with what matters. To you, your organization and its stakeholders. Some thoughts on what matters:
  - A mission that is meaningful… whether that is altruistic or creating

profit by delivering a needed or wanted product/service.

- Staying on mission... the organization continues to deliver on its mission.
- Deeper values... quality, customer satisfaction, stability, sustainability, leadership development.
- Delivering on the promises made to stakeholders... internal and external.

For larger organizations, these simple ideas can be difficult. The larger an organization, the more likely the branding is more about those things we mentioned earlier... the logo, the advertising, the tagline, etc. The running of the organization and the communicating of the brand can become disconnected. That's a subject for a consulting project (and if you run a large organization and want to connect organizational management, culture and brand efficacy, let me know... I'd be glad to help).

The smaller the organization, whom this book targets, has an easier time of developing and communicating the brand. Because the brand is you. The smaller the organization, the more the brand is about the people who work in the organization. From the owner to the person who greets prospects when they contact the company.

Let's explain that further with an example. Think about Coke. The logo, the script type Coca-Cola, the shape of the bottle, the polar bears, the look of the product as it tumbles over ice, and of course the taste... all these elements come to mind. They are meant to create connotations that are the brand: familiarity, refreshment, enjoyment, etc.

How many people do you know who work for Coke? For most of us, the answer is "zero". For some, it might be one or two. Then how do we know the Coke brand? The tens of millions of dollars the company has spent telling you about Coke, seeing the product and experiencing the product.

Now, let's think about your organization. Do you have millions of dollars telling people the attributes of your organization? (I hear your answer!)

So how do your current customers and prospects know your brand? Like Coke, some of their knowledge comes from experiencing the product (or service). They may recognize your logo from a brochure or letter (or invoice!), but probably, they know the brand because they know you and your staff or coworkers. If polled and your customers said "trustworthy" was an attribute of the company, they would only know that from their experience with you and your staff.

So let's reiterate some definitions:
1. The Brand is the collection of attributes of an organization and how those attributes are communicated.

2. The smaller the organization, the less the brand is about the creative and graphics and the more it is about the people within the organization. How they deliver the product or service and interact with prospects and customers.
3. Don't miss this: YOU ARE THE BRAND.

(At least until you get that marketing budget like Coke. :-)

Elements That Make Up A Brand

So if the way we do things and who we are help make up the brand, how do capture those ideas and attributes? How do you capture the essence of a company and then communicate it successfully? Let's look at a couple helpful frameworks for understanding your brand.

First, let's look at a breakdown of brand attributes. It is important to note, these are not intended to be judgments of your organization or brand. It is not wrong for an organization or product to fit one category or another… it is important to understand the category and within which your company/products fit.

Price – the cost of a product, or an organization's offering/product line, defines an important brand attribute. Whether we are the low-cost provider or are very expensive, defines a great deal of how we will operate, how the market perceives our company and products/service, and even what some of our other brand attributes will be.

Positioning – may follow price, but not necessarily. Positioning in the market as a boutique/specialty/custom provider versus a mass producer carries its own connotation no matter the price.

Perceived Value – how the market views the value of a product. Items that have a high perceived value may cost a few dollars, but their novelty, uniqueness, usefulness makes their perceived value very high.

True Value – differs from perceived value in that it takes the emotion (the perception) out of the value. An easy way to see the true value of something is to put it up for sale on eBay or at a garage sale.

Experience – what is the experience that goes along with the sale? Do we provide concierge level service or do we have simple, transactional sales?

Perspective – how does a customer's position change the view of our product/ service? As a result, do we have a niche appeal or universal?

Delivery System – how is our product delivered to the customer? How is it packaged? Shipped? Is it installed or self-serve?

Quality – along with price, the quality of our product is a key attribute. Products vary in quality (and they all have value for different reasons). How does our level of quality reflect on our organization and therefore the brand?

Communications – what type of communication do we have with our prospects and customers? Face-to-face? Relationship-driven? Via packaging only? In marketing communications (sales materials and advertising)?

Identity – what are the graphics and words that describe our organization? Logo, tagline, short descriptor… do these reflect the attributes of our brand?

Message – what is our message? From printed materials to the way we answer the phone or greet someone visiting our office or retail space… what is our message?

Media – where we advertise is also a key communicator of our brand.

Every organization has a brand…whether realized or not! "Everything" you do affects your brand. It must be strategically determined and communicated.

A second way to think about the brand is in the framework of equity to the customer. What value do different aspects of the brand communications hold? Following is a graphic that shows relative equity of elements of a brand.

Brand Equity Increases

Logo Tagline Content Look/Feel Experience

It is important to remember that the logo isn't the most important brand element. The experience customers have in the purchasing process and the post-sale experience of the product or service is the most important brand element. Our brand should reflect a wonderful experience that the customer has in acquiring and in using our product or service. Think of it this way: the value of the brand element increases as we move up the brand elements and the value of the brand should flow down and through the content we publish, our tagline and logo. The bottom line is that our brand is our customer's experience and our prospect's enticement.

Our Brand is our customer's experience AND our prospect's enticement.

We want the experience of buying to be so positive that it defines our brand as one the customer wants to experience again and to share with others. Every interaction with our customer must reinforce the good decision they made in hiring our firm, buying our product or service. This is how companies develop "fans" and "evangelists". These terms describe people who not only are glad they purchased a product or service, but are proud of their buying decision to the point of it being part of their identity. If you don't believe me, visit Pittsburgh on a Sunday.

While your brand may not result in apparel, you can develop your customer experience to the point of having fans. Fans who believe in your brand, are proud to be part of it, and share its value and virtues with others.

This sort of experience with a brand is what becomes attractive and enticing to prospects. Case studies, testimonials, reviews, referrals… the best of these come from brand fans.

At the end of this chapter are questions about the attributes of your brand. After you note the brand attributes, you'll be asked to determine which of these attributes are unique, or at least uncommon. Each organization is unique, and therefore, one, two or more things about your organization should help differentiate your brand from others.

A Commodity is Not A Commodity, and Service isn't Just Service

I was once asked by a customer who made a product that was basically a commodity item about this idea of unique brand attributes. If you make paper cups, how unique can you be? The reality is that even a product very similar to others is still made and delivered in a unique way.

It is imperative to understand this and to look seriously at your organization, its processes, people, and culture to determine what brand attributes are unique. It turns out my paper cup making friend had several unique advantages. One was being an early adopter of web-based automatic refill systems in their e-commerce functionality. Another was the people that worked in the customer service area. They were committed to not only fast response but were empowered to make decisions that other companies would only permit by senior management. These were attributes that created unique value.

How these attributes are communicated is also important. It is easy to say "we care about you", anyone can and most companies do. "We have great service" is like water in a world with over 2/3 of its surfaced covered in it. It has no meaning whatsoever.

To make our "great service" a unique attribute, it must:
- Be true. We must demonstrate it to be true in the customer's experience; and
- We must describe it at a level of detail that shows the uniqueness.

Do our customers tell us about how great our service is? How it is different than other companies? Does the email or phone call get answered live every time? A reply/solution sent within 24-hours? In other words, how is "great" defined? And while we're at it… can't we communicate it more factually and specifically?

"Our service team monitors text messages 24-hours-a-day and are empowered to solve any issue on the spot. Text this number to test them (number)."

That's a unique attribute for that company and should be a part of the brand communications and marketing message!

Your organization probably doesn't have that attribute. However, you do have unique attributes. Use the exercises following the chapter to work help find yours.

Roll It Into a USP

Once you have the unique attributes (or at least uncommon attributes), you can think about developing your Unique Selling Proposition. The USP is sort of like a 30-second elevator pitch of branding. It should answer the question of why a person or company would buy your services.

The Unique Selling Proposition should start with one statement that takes into account what matters to a company, why customers buy and the unique brand attributes. You are rolling up a lot of the work you've done into one statement.

CHAPTER 4
TAKEAWAYS AND EXERCISES

1. The brand is the amalgamation of the people, processes, products, communications and culture of an organization. It is the essence of the customer experience and prospects' enticement.

2. The smaller the organization, the more the brand is the people.

3. Consider how the people on your team affect the customer experience, and therefore, the brand.

   _____
   _____
   _____
   _____
   _____

4. What matters to leadership will speak volumes about the essence (the brand) of the organization.

5. Think about your organization as you did earlier about Mercedes Benz, McDonalds and the Steelers. What are the first ideas, images and words that come to mind?

   _____
   _____
   _____
   _____
   _____
   _____

6. What matters? What is the mission and values of your organization? Write what matters to you, your staff, your owners/board/shareholders and customers.

   _____
   _____
   _____
   _____
   _____
   _____

7. What are the attributes of your organization? Which directly come from who you are, how you deliver your product or service? Which are unique (or at least uncommon)? Use your answers from questions 1 & 2 to inform your list.

_____

_____

_____

_____

_____

_____

5
VALUE PROPOSITION

"(insert national news story here). No countians involved."

Providing Value

I have a friend who lives in a rural county with an old-style newspaper that focuses on local news. When he first moved to the county, he would jokingly tell of how the newspaper covered local stories with incredible depth but would simplify national and international news stories. Since the mission of the paper was to bring local news, they would qualify stories outside the region by determining if there was a local connection or not.

Your customers expect the same from your marketing. They want to know what connection they have with your marketing. In what we might consider more callous in other situations, your customer is asking a simple question: "What's in it for me?"

When you look at your client and prospect communications, look at it from the frame of reference of the client. That is easy to understand and difficult to do. There are many reasons for ineffective (or to state it directly, bad) marketing, and this reason is very common: we love our company, we love our product, we love our people… therefore we tell our story from our loving perspective.

Prospects don't share our love. Business-to-business prospects have a job to do and need to know how you are going to help them get that job done. Retail customers have wants and needs to fulfill, and they want to know your product or service can meet their need. So every time you look at your marketing think of your prospect saying, "What does that mean for me?".

Answer Their Question

Value Proposition answers that question. Most of us are familiar with the idea of value proposition (or sometimes called "sales proposition")… it is simply the true value we provide to customers. Sometimes it is tangible; often it is intangible. Value is a mix of features, benefits, the means, and the end. It can get complicated. So we'll try to break down the exercise of developing your value proposition (or plural "propositions" - see, it just got more complicated).

Fortunately, if we have gone through the exercises to this point in the Genius! Marketing process, we have the information we need to shape our value proposition:
- Attributes of prospects and customers
- Reasons people/companies buy
- Attributes of our organization that make it unique

This is the raw material for your value proposition. Like the earlier exercises, we want to uncover the unique. Let's look at a simple example: customer service.

Is Your Marketing Claim "Water"?

I used customer service as an example in the previous chapter about unique attributes. Let's look at it again as we define value proposition. Almost every company believes they provide good customer service. Plus, it is used countless times in advertising and marketing materials.

"We have great customer service."

That's great! You know what? "I love water."

These statements carry about the same level of meaning and impact. Let me explain why saying "We have great customer service" has absolutely no value as a marketing statement. Using my statement, "I love water".

Water is everywhere, from your driveway puddle to the great barrier reef. Water is in your sink, in your bottle, in your hair when it rains, and in your pool. It's at the beach, and it's frozen on the mountain, it rushes down in a stream, it flushes your toilet.

Before this becomes a Dr. Seuss parody, get the point: "Water" is meaningless.

For water to have meaning, I need to quantify it, focus my description or communicate more fully my meaning.

"Water is refreshing when I jump in the pool after mowing the lawn."

"Water adds so much to my experience hiking when it babbles in a brook next to a mountain trail."

"Water is critical so you don't scorch the bottom of the pot when you're making this recipe."

Any of these (and many more) could be the reason that "I love water."

It's the same with customer service. If your marketing says "We have great customer service", it may just as well say "We have customer service". Yes, and the ocean is wet. Every company has customer service. And just about every company claims its customer service is great.

When you say it, you should hear your customer thinking, "What does that mean to me?".

Make it Meaningful; Then you have Value
What is your claim about customer service? What does your company do to make your customer service "great"? Look for the value to the customer. Look for the unique. Look for what matters.

"Our service pledge is this: if you're not satisfied with your experience, let an associate know, and the president of our company will contact you to discuss your issue and make it right."

Now that's a customer service statement that is a value proposition. Doesn't even compare with a typical "we have great service" line, does it? It communicates attributes of an organization (Branding chapter), why a customer buys (Reason for Sales chapter), and who our customers are (Assessment chapter). The real values communicated are:
- Listening
- Access
- Redress

And more. That's what a value proposition needs to do: reflect who you are as a company and what you do for a customer that the customer defines as valuable.

...reflect who you are as a company and what you do for a customer that the customer defines as valuable.

Couple things to note: 1) you don't necessarily have to have a customer service value proposition, so don't get hung up on this example; and 2) a value proposition doesn't need to be as grandiose as that customer service statement. Let's look at some other ways to communicate value.

Features, Benefits, Value

Often a simple feature or benefit can make a dynamite value prop. A pharmacy open 24-hours provides real value to a customer with a bad cold and no medicine or chicken soup. It can go unstated (because the pharmacy assumes the recognition of value) but it would also make a nice line in a marketing message:

"Don't sweat not having the medicine you need when you need it… we're open and have a licensed pharmacist on duty 24-hours a day." That answers the "What's in it for me?" question.

Likewise, a benefit can turn into a value prop. One of the benefits my consulting clients enjoy is that they no longer have to worry about managing their marketing. I help them by taking on the role of VP of Marketing or Marketing Director. That's a benefit. They may still ask, "What's that mean to me?". My answer is this value proposition:

"When you hire Eckert to serve as your virtual VP of Marketing, you won't have to worry about the day-to-day planning or implementation of your marketing. You'll receive regular reports on progress, see all marketing for final approval before publication, and receive the communication you need to keep internal stakeholders (like managers and board) aware and coordinated."

The "What's in it for me?" is apparent to a busy CEO or business owner.

Make it Valuable!

There is value in a feature. There is value in a benefit. The (often intangible) true value to the customer is that your product or service solves a problem, ends a headache, saves significant money, increases productivity, etc.

Instead of assuming your prospects know the value your feature or benefit brings, make it clear by turning it into a value proposition:

Our new cutting machine has 20% faster relay time. (Feature)
So there are no delays in production at this step in the manufacturing process. (Benefit)
That means more deliverable goods every shift, every day. (Value Prop - answers the "What's in it for me?" question.)
So if you're generating 10 units per minute and change to this cutting machine, it can increase to 12 per minute which lowers production cost due to reduced labor costs by $350 per day. (Proof – The best value propositions are quantifiable.)

Walk the prospect through the value, don't leave it up to chance that they will "get it". People are busy, and it's your marketing's job to make sure the prospect knows the value of buying from your organization.

Proof

Showing proof in a value proposition should be easy to do. Often it's not. It should be easy because if you are going to make a claim about your product or service, that means the value described is value your company delivers... and that value should be easy to articulate. However, not every situation is like the manufacturing example above... not every value is quantifiable in a number, as a cost or in a percentage.

Quantifiable proof is excellent, but anecdotal proof can be sufficient as well. Below are a few value propositions that do not have quantifiable proof, but are very compelling because the evidence is a real example, a customer testimonial, and a third-party endorsement.

1. An Insurance Agency
We help our clients from beginning to end with insurance claim issues so that they can focus on getting well and not worrying about claim payment.
In one case, our dedicated claims representatives were able to pinpoint a coding error made at the doctor's office, which avoided many potential billing complications for our customer.

2. A Landscaping Company
By manicuring a lawn and garden on a regular schedule,
the busy homeowner doesn't have to worry how her lawn looks and it is always ready for guests and outdoor activities.
"They are great. My lawn is beautiful, and I love knowing that when I get home from work, I can enjoy my backyard and garden without doing a thing!" - Jennifer L.

3. A Bank
Our loan officer will guide you through financing your first home purchase; she'll help you gather all the information and explain each step in the process so you can feel confident you won't miss out when you find your dream home.
Our team won the gold (first place) in the community choice award category for the best mortgage lender.

These examples communicate value very well, even though they do not include numbers. The proof is in a case example, a testimonial, and a third-party recognition. When using these techniques, it is important to have the full story available should a prospect ask about the value claim. That could be a longer form case history on a website, in a PDF or a page of testimonials. Awards or other recognition plaques or icons are popular ways to show third-party recognition. The salesforce must also be aware of how to answer a question about examples used in marketing materials or advertising.

Form and Function

You may notice in the examples in this chapter that value proposition can be formulaic. When I work with a customer on value proposition, we work on developing value propositions in a fairly rigid way. We start with three types:

Value about the company

Value for products or services

Value about brand attributes

Each potential value proposition is "built" using this formula:

What it is… Often it is a feature, but it could be a brand attribute.

How it helps… Typically is a benefit received by the customer, which could be tangible or intangible (the way the customer feels).

Proof… Gives an example, data or makes the case.

In the examples, you could see this formula in the wording such as:

"We help…",

"So that…",

"In one case…"

Use such a formula when initially building your value propositions. After you have a set of props for your business, products, and brand in this format, they can be altered and used in different narratives and messages. The format will help you build a "language" of value proposition with your sales team or staff. Engage them to write their value props which can be used in sales pitches, marketing messages and on the company website.

It is beneficial to have all staff aware of the true value the organization provides. Enlisting them in the process of building value propositions will reinforce to everyone the value provided. It will also create a more rounded library of value props, as each area of an organization delivers value in different ways.

CHAPTER 5
TAKEAWAYS AND EXERCISES

1. You must prove to the prospect (and the customer) the value your company, brand and product/service provides.

2. Look back at your answers in the earlier chapters of this book. Use the formula to begin building value proposition.

   The What "We help…"

   _____

   The Help "So that the customer…"

   _____

   Proof "The result…"

   _____

3. Meet with staff or other stakeholders to review your value propositions and brainstorm other value that the organization provides to customers.

6
THE MESSAGE

One night only! Limited time offer! Not available in stores!
All the rage in the U.K.!

You won't be surprised at this point in the book that the answers from the exercises earlier in the book will be used in the marketing message. One of the principles of Genius! Marketing is that the marketing flows from what and who the organization is. Marketing is the embodiment of the organization. The concept of False Advertising should not exist because the marketing message should naturally flow from the organization and its brand.

Why make things up when you have a unique company, do things in your own way, serve customers with people that no one else can and provide an experience to customers that is one of a kind?

That said, marketing communications don't write and design themselves! Copywriters, graphic designers, and programmers can all play a part in creating advertising and marketing communications. However, the message is best when it is developed by the people that care the most, the people that serve the customer, deliver the product… are a part of the organization.

It starts with the business owner or senior management which is setting the strategy and financial goals for the company. Those goals and the work done in chapters 1 - 5 should drive the marketing message. The message can be turned over to designers and creatives to shape the final advertising product, but the message should start with you.

To that end, let's look at the content pyramid. The content pyramid is designed to help develop the narrative content for marketing communications elements. It can be worked from widest to narrow or vice versa. The goal is to develop as much content as possible at the wide end and at the narrow, to communicate the same brand identity in just a few words. This is a difficult but key task...to consistently deliver the organization's unique selling proposition, brand and 'personality' through all communications and media no matter how short. Not every tweet can tell the whole story… but it should tell a part of it. Or at a minimum point to it.

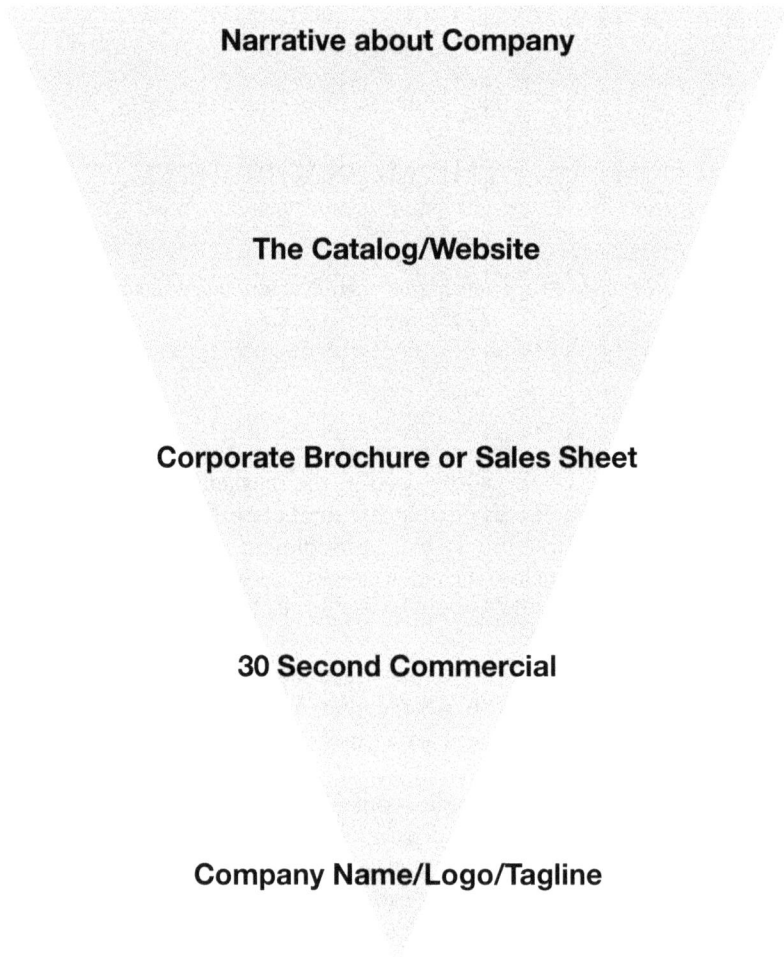

Narrative about Company

The Catalog/Website

Corporate Brochure or Sales Sheet

30 Second Commercial

Company Name/Logo/Tagline

Let's start with the wide end of the pyramid.

Narrative About the Company
A multiple page document that may begin as a "stream of thoughts" narrative or a list of attributes. It will describe the business, products, strategy, operations… anything that helps express who and what the business is and does. This is where

you write from everyone's perspective:
- ✓ Show your pride in your company
- ✓ Overview or history plus why you're in business
- ✓ Describe how your operation works
- ✓ Perspective of staff and employees – working for the company
- ✓ How the organization is unique
- ✓ Why people buy
- ✓ Problems you solve
- ✓ Advantages of working with the organization
- ✓ Describe brand attributes and "the intangibles"
- ✓ Give examples of customers' good experiences
- ✓ Make your value proposition

Just keep writing...

This can come easily to some people, however, I understand how daunting a task it can be. So here is an exercise that I use to help people get in the "write" frame of mind!

The Letter to Your Roommate
Write a letter to your college roommate or another long lost friend. Someone you haven't talked to in a while, but the type who you'd pick up the relationship immediately if you had the opportunity to do so. Start the letter this way...

Dear (name),

It's been too long. I just wanted to tell you about the work I am doing now and the great organization with which I've had the opportunity to be associated.

Then write...

In this situation, you would write in a familiar but detailed way. A friend who may know nothing about your company, your product or even how a company runs... but one who would be interested.

This exercise works because it puts you in a different frame of mind than having to work on your marketing. Not that marketing isn't fun, but it is a work task. This writing should be fun.

A question I get: "Shouldn't I write for an audience that doesn't know my company? And possibly is wary of my business?"

In a word, "no". To take that tack will result in statements and a style that is not natural. When you talk to someone who is wary, it can cause you to press your points or feel pressured to perform. Writing to an interested individual will let the essence of your organization flow in the narrative. No defensiveness, just honest, passionate description of your work and your organization.

Write as much as you can. Go into detail. The idea of the pyramid is to put plenty of ideas in the top and then pick and choose the narrative that stays as less and less space is available in the communications elements further down the pyramid.

When you have this long narrative, plus the answers to the exercises in the first five chapters, you can then turn it over to a marketing consultant (like me), or a designer or agency. They can help you decide which messaging works its way into your marketing communications.

Couple Tips for Writing

The letter exercise helps because it sets a context for why you're writing. It helps the words flow more naturally, but here are some additional tips for writing your letter/narrative.

Explain… a lot. Don't assume your audience understands your business. Don't use jargon (unless you explain it). Don't assume, when you assume it makes…

Write from both sides. Write about your personal and your team's passion. Also, write from the prospect/customer needs and desires.

Payoff your value props. We developed short statements for value propositions in the last chapter, explain them more fully (give examples, give proofs, tell your story) in this narrative.

Think about the mall. A spray of perfume. A taste of high-end chocolate. And other samples to try out products. Your marketing message should be like that: giving your prospects a small "taste" of what your customers experience.

Include quotes. It helps to have testimonials, quotes and third-party confirmation (awards, certifications, etc.) of your claims.

Put the pain and the experience together. Connecting the pain (reasons people buy), the solution (your product or service) and the how the solution feels (as well as the results) is the best way to convince prospects that they need to learn more.

Tell a story. Whether you write marketing narrative about your company or use the letter exercise, the goal is to capture the unique story of your organization, what makes it special, and how it can help other people with certain needs and wants. It doesn't need to be perfect grammatically. It doesn't need to be perfect advertising copy. It does need to be as complete as possible.

Once you have finished writing your narrative about your company (or your letter), consider letting a few people read it and ask the question: "How accurately does this portray the organization and its mission?" Once you're satisfied with the narrative, you can start to apply it.

Application of the Message

It would be great if you could expect your prospects (and customers) to read your full story, but the reality is that everyone is busy and few take the time to read long-form narratives. People want the information they want, when they want it and the ability to access more as they need it. It is our jobs as Genius! Marketers to provide this service to them. As we move down the content pyramid, we start to shape the amount and type of information we share through varying marketing communications. (Contact me if you need help with applying your story to your marketing.)

The Catalog (a.k.a. The Website)

Back in the day, many companies had catalogs. The catalog was where you told the whole story. Some companies still do have catalogs (like the clothing retailers who still clog mailboxes on a seemingly daily basis) but these aren't the kind of catalogs I'm talking about. The Sears Roebuck or JC Penney catalogs of yesteryear or in the industrial world the Grainger or WESCO catalogs. They had EVERYTHING in them. They were the mobile version of the retail store and were the reference guide that was always nearby whenever a need arose.

Today, the catalog is the website. You literally have unlimited space to tell your story. It's even better than the old school catalog because it can be changed at any time. The website should have an organized and detailed description of the products, benefits and unique attributes of the company, but now beginning to focus on the prospective buyer and/or other stakeholders.

The key is organizing it in a way that makes it easy for the reader to find the information they need. In a catalog, there were sections, categories, and subcategories. On your website, you want to supply the most critical information (for the most impatient site visitors) in a quick and easy way to get the buying information they need, and then organize information for people who require research and analysis before making a purchase.

As you review your message narrative, begin to place your content into these buckets:
- Core content that can be summarized or in bullet form
- Detailed information that will be linked from the core information

There are many ways to organize a website, but this is the best starting point: What is critical and what is the detail that explains the critical? Then it can be organized further by the best practices of web design: about, products, proofs, process and connection. (Contact Genius! Marketing if you are interested in learning more about website organization.)

Since a website has unlimited space, you could include everything you have in your messaging narrative, however, as you organize and prioritize the messages for application, some messaging may become superfluous for the external audience: prospect and customer.

The website tells "the whole story", it goes as deep as we'd like in one place. I like to say that the website is where we can provide the entire marketing conversation in one place for consumption at one time by our audience (if they choose). The Marketing Calendar is where we take the conversation and deliver it over time to our audiences. We'll discuss the Marketing Calendar in a later chapter.

One way to work through the "cut down" process is to highlight your long narrative. Possibly use different colors or designations (A, B, C…) to prioritize the long content for use on a website, in the brochure or the 30-second commercial.

The Corporate Brochure

At this stage, the message is reworked to fit the parameters of a printed piece and the (low) attention span of a suspect (someone who could be a prospect but isn't in our pipeline). The message now focuses on the unique selling proposition and benefits. Whether a multiple page brochure or a "mini-brochure" (one sheet folded twice into a #10 envelope size brochure), there is limited space. The brochure is used typically as a sales call leave behind, at a show or other prospecting use, as an outbound mailing, or as a follow up to an inquiry.

With a brochure you want to tell as much of the story as possible, but due to space, only the most pertinent information will fit. A mini-brochure is full of copy at 1,900 words. So take from your long narrative only the key elements that will engage the reader and have them interested in more information. That means focusing clearly on the offer, its value and the uniqueness of your organization.

The brochure may also become multiple pieces if there are multiple and disparate products or services or divisions within your company.

The 30 Second Commercial

Sometimes called the elevator pitch, this is the dinner party answer to the question, "What do you do?". It must carry the company message, but be delivered in a concise, clear and compelling manner. It also could be a 30-second commercial script for radio or TV or online video.

I will often also use it as the first/introductory paragraph to longer narratives.

Like the brochure, you may have a series of 30-second scripts to tell different parts of the story or to frame the story to a particular suspect/prospect/customer perspective. For one elevator pitch or 30-second script, communicate one idea. Pick out a few of the most important points you wrote in your long narrative and craft them into elevator pitches. Or, consider choosing one value proposition from the previous chapter to develop one script. Work through what is most important to say in a short time to an important audience.

The Tagline

The Content Pyramid graphic lists "Company Name/Logo/Tagline". We'll focus on the tagline here because 1) the company probably already has a name, and 2) we're working on the message, not graphic design. The logo can and should reflect the company brand and attributes. (Let me know if you are looking to develop a logo, I know some great graphic designers.)

Likewise, the tagline might be best written by a professional. Having external perspective is very helpful when trying to capture the essence of a company in five words or less. However, it never hurts to work on writing a tagline or a few… even if you hire a marketing consultant or copywriter. It can help with the creative process to understand what the owner/CEO/management team believes is the best way to describe the company in one line.

This is where consuming advertising can be helpful. Large companies spend large sums of money on creative including the development of a tagline. It is important to get "right" because it should represent the organization for a long time.

Companies also develop a tagline for advertising campaigns, which don't have the longevity and may focus on a message for a particular audience or offer.

Review your narrative and the highlights you made. What words stand out? Think about what mattered most in the earlier exercises. Think about the words and note ideas that come. Sometimes a good line is apparent immediately. Sometimes it takes time and reflection. Either way, give it a shot.

Disclaimer: if you use external creative resources, they may or may not like your ideas. Don't take this emotionally. Listen, try to understand the logic in their creatives. Ultimately, though, you and your team must decide on the line that works for your company, your people, and your audience.

Three Parts to a Strong Message

At any length, a strong marketing message considers who the audience is and their needs and wants… what the "pain" is that they are feeling that your product or service can solve. Use these three parts, each focused on the target reader/viewer to simply and effectively deliver your message.

1. Orienting Statement

This is the introduction to your message. It should orient the reader to what you want to communicate. It could come in the form of a clear statement or a teasing question.

"Homeowners can save money by combining car and home insurance." This statement tells who the message is for (audience), why they would be interested (benefit) and how they attain it (feature).

A question can also be a good orienting statement, but it should be a question to which it is not easy to answer "No".

"Need a break? Consider a weekend at the Lakehouse Lodge where everyone relaxes." This question would be difficult to turn down and a positive reaction would lead the audience to consider the next statement.

2. Explanation

The explanation may be like the "so that" statement in the value proposition. It may further explain the benefit or result of the product or service. It could also be a proof. The goal is to move the audience from the orienting statement to the call to action. Give some reason why the orienting statement is true and why the reader should take the next step.

"Homeowners can save money by combining car and home insurance. That's why XYZ Insurance will review all your insurance and make sure you have the right coverages, then we'll show you the cost savings when you combine home and auto."

"Need a break? Consider a weekend at the Lakehouse Lodge where everyone relaxes. No one can resist our couples massage lake cruise. Or try our double dip floating ice cream parlor. That's why we're rated 4.95 out of 5 on lakereview.com."

Once the audience knows the message is for them, and the reason why they should buy, it is time to move them to action.

3. Call to Action

It is important to consider the next step when developing messaging. If someone takes the time to read a sales sheet or brochure, goes to your website or looks at a social media page… then what? A clear call-to-action is necessary to get an action to be taken. The shorter the marketing message, such as a brochure or the next step down the pyramid, the commercial, it becomes more important to direct the reader/viewer to the next step.

Calls to action vary from the ultimate step (Buy Now!) to intermediary steps to the sale. Common calls to action are to buy now, get a free information kit, provide specifications for a project, have an estimate done and try for a free test period.

For simple and low-cost sales, "buy" is typically the call to action. The more complex, costly or technical the purchase, the more steps in the sales process. At each step, there will be a call to action to help move the prospect to the next step. Review the sample process flow chart and your process exercises in chapter 3 and consider calls to action for each step in the sale process.

When developing your marketing materials, consider the call to action and how it fits in as the conclusion of the information provided in the marketing piece. When you develop multiple versions for differing prospect/customer segments the call to action may be different. The goal is to make the step as easy to take as possible, relevant to the audience and their buying process and if possible valuable or urgent.

"Homeowners can save money by combining car and home insurance. That's why XYZ Insurance will review all your insurance and make sure you have the right coverages, then we'll show you the cost savings when you combine home and auto. Call 800-XYZ-1234 to talk to a rep about our situation or visit xyzinsurance.com for our anonymous quote estimator."

"Need a break? Consider a weekend at the Lakehouse Lodge where everyone relaxes. No one can resist our couples massage lake cruise. Or try our double dip floating ice cream parlor. That's why we're rated 4.95 out of 5 on lakereview.com. Visit lakehouselodgeinfo.com to see beautiful photos and review available rooms and cabins for your next stay."

Neither of these scripts tells the audience directly to buy. Each lays out what the offer is in the orienting statement, then gives some reason why the offer solves a problem and closes with an easy next step.

Get to It!

While developing messaging can be difficult, you as owner or manager are the first, best person to be thinking through what the organization should say. As mentioned earlier, don't worry about it being perfect – either in content or grammar. Use a professional as needed to polish and finish your messaging. Remember: your organization is unique and you have a unique story to tell. So review the exercises from earlier in the book, and start writing!

CHAPTER 6
TAKEAWAYS AND EXERCISES

1. Great marketing messages come from what matters to the organization and the audience. Focus on value.

2. The long narrative or letter writing exercise is a first step to developing great marketing content.

3. Review and prioritize what you write to help you or creative professionals develop great marketing materials and advertising.

4. The best messages are simple with an orienting statement, explanation and call to action.

5. Your exercise: write your long narrative!
    a. Write your letter or long narrative.
    b. Have someone you trust review it.
    c. Highlight and prioritize for website, brochure, commercial and tagline.
    d. Engage a designer or other creative team.

7
CHOOSING MARKETING TACTICS

Ideas are a dime a dozen.

Everybody loves marketing tactics. I work with a company at which the CFO takes every opportunity to take a shot at the "fun" marketing committee. He once slapped a handmade sign on the glass door of the conference room I was in: "Marketing meeting, Two drink minimum." He was wrong of course; it was an open bar…

Marketing is serious strategic and tactical work, but it is often thought of as "fun" because people enjoy creativity and brainstorming ideas. As we discussed earlier in the book, people also like marketing because they believe they already know how to do it since they have experienced so much marketing in their personal and professional lives.

So, we must be on guard as we develop our tactics list to not chase after the fun, the cool, the latest, etc. We need our tactics to have one purpose and one purpose only: to support our company strategic, sales and financial goals.

Start Your List
Earlier in the book, in the first and second chapter, we talked about ideas. Exercises included making a list of ideas for our marketing tactics and writing down all the marketing we are doing already. Have those lists handy.

Perhaps you already have a long list of tactics that you have launched or are currently running. Maybe you have a very long list of new ideas as well. If that's the case, you can probably skip the next section about developing ideas.

Not all organizations with which I work have a lot of ideas. Sometimes, rarely, they have no ideas about marketing. These companies usually come in two varieties: either they are not comfortable coming up with marketing ideas (I worked with an engineering firm which was self-aware enough to know they were excellent engineers, but not marketers) or they want a (so-called) Marketing Genius to tell them what ideas will work.

While I am comfortable working with non-creatives (the engineers were great to work with) and being called a Marketing Genius(!), I still endeavor to engage the ownership, management and staff (if appropriate) in the marketing brainstorming and planning process. After all, as I stated earlier, it is the people in the company from which the unique attributes and brand flow. So with the marketing ideas as well.

Developing Ideas
If you have a team from which you can solicit ideas about your marketing, you may want to schedule a work session about marketing. You could review some of the work you've done assessing and defining your organization and its brand. Share the messaging you've written.

Then permit the team to brainstorm ideas. They all (more or less, nod to the engineers) will have ideas to share. However, whether you are coming up with all the ideas yourself as the owner of the company, or you are holding a company-wide brainstorming session, there are a few ground rules.

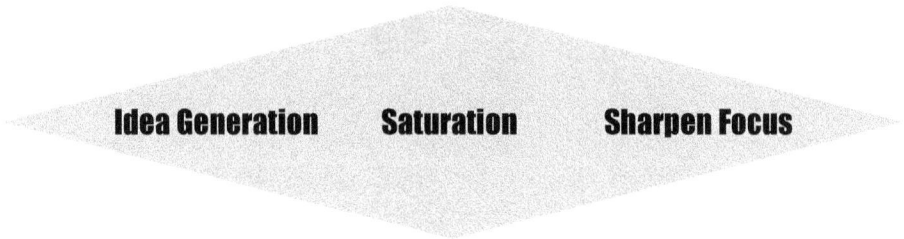

Idea Generation   Saturation   Sharpen Focus

1. No Judgment
I like to use the diamond method of brainstorming and organizing ideas. As the diamond graphic shows, generate ideas to saturation before judgment. Make clear in a brainstorming session that all ideas are welcome, and that no one is permitted to judge an idea or be negative.

That said, also make sure that everyone understands that phase one is idea generation, but there is a phase two, which includes moving from ideas to projects. Projects do require judgment and have other constraining factors. Constraints could consist of how well the idea will engage the target audience or if the idea fits into the sales process and can help move a suspect or prospect to the next step in the buying process. There also could be budget related constraints.

During the brainstorming session, don't judge. Just write the ideas down. When people start to judge, stop them and remind them that there is a phase two for looking at ideas versus the constraints. After all, this is probably a new experience for your staff, so be open and encouraging. Plus, people tend to give ideas with a reason, so they are prejudging their idea as a good one or at least one that deserves consideration. Don't squash it… yet. Don't let others squash it, either.

2. Focus the Discussion
Ideas usually come in the form of tactics, meaning you will hear things like:

"We should do an email newsletter."
"PR is free. Let's get a story in the local news about our company."
"We should start a Facebook page for the company."
"I saw an ad for (Competitor Company) on a billboard. Why don't we do that?"

These are all tactics. We are looking for ideas for tactics. However, as you brainstorm, remind participants (or yourself if you are doing this on your own) to also give ideas for subjects to promote and messages for the marketing. Get them thinking about unique attributes and value propositions as well as tactics. It's not all about the media through which you deliver your message. It's about the content: value props, benefits, attributes, etc. Ask questions to prompt discussion about the company, its products, operations and other less tangible assets of the organization.

The result will be that you get both: ideas for tactics and ideas to fill the tactics with meaningful content.

3. Follow-Up
Use follow-up questions to get people talking and to direct the conversation.

"What matters most to our customers?"
"Why do people buy from us?"
"What is the hidden gem that nobody knows about our company?"
"If we launch a (insert tactic here), what should the message be?"
"When you're buying, what marketing do you use to inform your purchase?"
"Do the sales tools we have now work well? What is missing?"

You may learn quite a bit which you can consider adding to the work you've done earlier on brand and message. And you'll have a long list of tactics.

How to Judge the Ideas
The ideas that you develop through the process of reading this book or a brainstorming session may not be used in your short-term marketing plan. Some may be held in reserve for future marketing plans; some may be discarded for varying reasons.

1. Priorities

In all areas of life, there are things with higher priority and things with lower priority. This is true of marketing as well. When brainstorming it is easy to gravitate to the latest, hippest ideas. Or to focus on the ideas that the competition or other famous brands are using. These tactics may not be right for your plan. Rather, prioritize tactics that have the best opportunity to help reach your company, strategic and financial goals.

Some companies prioritize sales in their marketing. The sole purpose of marketing is to support the sales process. Other companies are looking to grow sales, but also build and communicate a brand, build awareness or grow the company's name recognition in a new marketplace.

Each of these goals could result in different tactics, with different marketing messages and focus on different organizational attributes and value props. For sales focus, a strong value proposition and call to action is the highest priority. When targeting brand awareness, the reach of the media (the ability to have the marketing message heard or seen by the most people) will be a higher priority.

Prioritize the tactics you will work on first based on their likely effectiveness in helping your organization reach its most important goals.

2. Tie to Resources

Later in this book, we will discuss marketing resources. Most notably budget. Budget is a constraining factor. However, not just money budget, but time budget, energy budget, and skill set budget.

There are ideas that are just "a bridge too far".

"Let's unfurl a huge banner of our logo in space that can be seen from earth." (This was actually an idea considered by a few big brands a decade or so ago.) Fun idea… probably too far out to keep on the list.

If an idea in the brainstorming session is "Start our own TV show", you probably won't want to spend the money, time, have the energy or the skill set to make that idea a reality. That said, you can write it down during the brainstorming session and judge it unrealistic later. Or modify it due to constraining factors ("We can't do a TV show on network TV right now, but what if we did a video blog?").

3. If/Then

It is not wrong to have really big ideas. For marketing or for your business in general.

"We'd like to advertise during the super bowl."

Could be a great idea for your company. Another constraining factor is when you can take on an idea. You may be able to set aside an idea based on things that must happen before the idea can become a reality. Consider it a stretch goal, don't spend time and energy on it, but put a few markers down.

"If we get the second round of funding, have sales of $10,000,000 annually and operate in at least 30 states, we'll consider a super bowl ad."

4. Tie to Process
When considering ideas for inclusion in your plan, think about where they fit. Is the message or the media best for suspects (people who we don't have in our database, but could be prospects) and therefore early in our marketing process? Would it be the kind of message and media that would be best used to help move prospects through the last steps of the sales process towards the close? Maybe you have a message that needs to be communicated throughout the whole marketing/sales process. Maybe you have one media that reaches every suspect, prospect and customer. I doubt it, though.

An example: "We want one brochure that will tell our whole story."

That's great, and there is no reason not to have a piece that tells your whole story (like the website as we described it earlier). That said, how many times have you seen a potential customer (you, for instance), ignore the marketing information and pieces in a proposal packet? At that point in the process, a prospect has vetted the company, probably seen the brochure before, and looked at a lot of information on the website or elsewhere about the company. There is nothing wrong with including a company brochure with the proposal. Maybe someone who hasn't done the research will end up reviewing the proposal and the brochure in the proposal packet makes sense. Often though, it is ignored and filed away or tossed.

Another example: "We want to use email because it can reach all of our prospects and customers."

True. Email is great to help prospects get more information to move forward in the sales process or to remind customers of their great purchase decision (buying from you) and provide them with opportunities to buy again. That said, I just segmented the email into two tactics or at least two sets of messages within emails to two target audiences. Tying the tactic and the message to the steps in the process is important to tighten the message, organize the audience into manageable groups and make the tactic more effective.

While we won't go deeply into the idea of one-to-one customization of marketing in this book (that will be covered in the tactic resource guide being developed), you must consider your target audience or personae and the best way to reach them with the best message for where they are in the steps that are the selling process.

4. New isn't Always Better

When determining which tactics will be a part of your short list, don't assume new ideas are better than old ones. Meaning this: remember that you probably are already doing some marketing now. You have a brochure, an email newsletter, ads, whatever. Make sure you judge that list as well. Perhaps some of your best ideas are already part of your marketing mix but haven't been executed well. Maybe your current tactics need an update or can be repositioned to a different audience or step in the selling process. Don't assume new ideas are better than what you have going on now. Maybe you just aren't doing the current tactics correctly. (Sorry, somebody had to say it!)

How Long a List?

Your "judged" (or better "prioritized") list shouldn't be too long. The longer the list, the more likely it needs to be segmented further or categorized further. Also the more likely you'll never get it done. (Let's be honest here!)

I like to have my customers start with the 1, 2, 3 most important things for the short-term plan. If there was only one thing we could do, what would it be? Then what? Then what? Our top three priorities.

That's just practical experience talking.

If you have a list of 6 - 12 things you want to accomplish over the next marketing year, that's fine. We will be incorporating them into our action plan which looks at tactics over time… in other words, when will we accomplish items 1, 2, 3 and so on. They can't (read that as won't) all happen at the same time.

CHAPTER 7
TAKEAWAYS AND EXERCISES

1. Ideas are a dime a dozen. Tactics take good execution to be effective.

2. Brainstorm ideas or review your list of tactics from earlier in the book.

3. If you brainstorm with your team, don't judge the ideas and lead the discussion to include not only tactical ideas but ideas about content, brand, audience and more (all those will help with good execution of the tactic).

4. If you could only do one tactic, it would be:

   _____

   The second priority is:

   _____

   The third priority is:

   _____

5. Where in the marketing/sales process will these tactics best fit?

   _____
   _____
   _____

6. What audience would these tactics best fit?

   _____
   _____
   _____

Stephen L. Eckert

8
RESOURCES

Freedom is Not Free... Neither is Social Media.

Neither is PR. That's a fact. One of the most frustrating things for a marketer is for non-marketers to assume things can be done for free or very low cost. I have been told by companies that they want to use PR or Social Media because "it's free". Advertising, conversely, is "expensive".

Not free. More difficult to track cost, but not free. There are four main types of cost when it comes to marketing:

1. Budget/Money
2. People/Time
3. Energy
4. Expertise

Let's look at a couple of examples.

Advertising: Expensive
If we were to talk for ten minutes while I look at your website, I could place a Google search ad for your business in less than an hour. I could write, produce and place a radio ad for your business in three hours. There would be a cost to the media - setting a budget with Google and a cost to the radio airtime. Each would show up as an invoice or charge on your credit card at the end of the month. That's a marketing tactic that "costs" or is "expensive".

PR: Free
To place a PR story with a local publication or media outlet, I'd need to

understand your company, talking to management or key players about the subject of the news release and possibly need to have a photograph shot (some news outlets require a photo with releases). Together, we would develop a news release and list of subjects for media consideration.

The news release would be distributed electronically and possibly picked up by a publication or online news or industry source. The subjects for news stories or features are pitched to media contacts which would include email, mail and possibly phone follow up. Potentially a visit by a journalist to your site would be scheduled with an interview. A feature story would probably include a photo session and submitting resource information whether specs, logos or other graphics.

Could end up as a nice story about your company, or at least being a part of a larger story the journalist publishes. No invoice comes at the end of the month (except mine if I helped you with the news release and media pitch and the distribution service cost). Additionally, how much soft cost was spent on the project? From your time talking to the media to taking photos to staff cleaning up before the media visit?

Couple Disclaimers:
1. I'd like to know your company a little better than a ten-minute phone call before placing an ad. I could do it that quickly though, and it probably would be marginally successful.

2. Also, I'm not saying PR is bad. PR and Social Media can be a very productive part of the marketing tactic mix. This discussion is just about cost. PR costs plenty. Social Media costs some budget/money (developing content, graphics, video, etc.), but it is a substantial cost in time, energy and expertise.

Developing Your Budgets

Remember the marketing process map developed earlier? It is the key to developing the budget (money) and understanding needs in the other areas (time, energy, expertise). For our purposes, we will simplify the process into four steps. You will have more steps.

Example Steps in Selling Process:
1. Qualified Lead
2. Meeting/Specifications
3. Estimate/Proposal
4. Close/Contract

The steps will have different names depending on the industry.

The first step is to start with the desired result, or in other words, your goal. It could be a dollar amount, items or projects sold, the number of customers gained or other goal.

Example: XYZ Service Company sets a goal of 50 projects sold in the year

We want to fill in a number for each step in the pipeline. We will create a pipeline with four steps (you can do this on paper or in a spreadsheet). On the left is performance meaning what we can expect or know is the reality. Our actual performance. On the right side is our goal - what we need at each step of the process to reach our bottom line annual goal.

Performance	Step in Process	Goal
	Leads	
	Meeting/Specs	
	Estimate/Proposal	
1	Close/Contract	50

The XYZ goal of 50 projects sold for the year is added to the bottom row in the Goal column.

From this point, the numbers on the goal side are added based on our performance numbers. We reverse engineer how many leads XYZ will need based on the real numbers from the performance column. So, step two (after setting the goal) is to know your numbers. For some companies (I hope yours) the numbers are easy to access. For others, it may be more difficult.

How many estimates are provided to get one closed project at XYZ? Based on feedback from the salesforce or data we track in our prospecting system or customer relationship management software, the number is five. Five is entered on the left track in the "Estimate/Proposal" row. Multiply the goal by that number to fill in the goal side of the pipeline. Start tracking your numbers in each step of the process. For the first time through, it may take some data diving, conversations with the sales team or maybe, just an educated guess. It's okay not to know. Start tracking or mining these numbers from the information you have and improve the system and the forecast as you move forward each planning cycle.

Next, how many calls are needed to generate the number of estimates on the performance side. Again, you may not know this number, but let's say it is 20 meetings to get five estimates. That is a multiplier of four, so fill in the goal side number of estimates (250 times 4) to determine the goal for calls for the year.

Then on the top line, add in the performance side number for the number of leads or inquiries to generate 20 meetings with a prospect. XYZ Company meet with 50% of the people that inquire. So the number is added as 40 leads or inquiries needed at the top of the sales process. On the goal side, two times the goal for meetings is the number of inquiries or leads needed, or 2,000.

XYZ Service Company's sales numbers:

Performance	Step in Process	Goal
40	Leads	2000
20	Meeting/Specs	1000
5	Estimate/Proposal	250
1	Close/Contract	50

It is clear now, based on past performance by the sales process that 2,000 leads are needed to reach the goal of 50 new projects. This begs the question: How does XYZ attain 2,000 leads?

On to the marketing part of the process. The goal of the marketing tactics is to yield 2,000 leads or inquiries.

In the case of XYZ, their marketing includes their website, direct mail, email, word of mouth and other sources of inquiries.

We begin by assigning how many leads each marketing tactic yields. Real life isn't as clean as this example, since you don't always know from where every lead comes, and suspects and target audiences may receive more than one type of marketing tactic. You can decide how to assign the number of leads. Tracking some marketing tactics is easier than others. One reason digital advertising is popular is because it is easy to track and see the results.

Assigning Source

As you deploy marketing tactics, consider how to track them. At worst, ask prospects how they found your company and if they remember hearing, seeing or clicking an ad. This will yield some data. There are ways to track most advertising - use a coupon in print, have a unique phone number for radio, use landing pages and lead offers on websites and with digital ads and email. Broadcasters even track online activity – determining web traffic within the first few minutes following the broadcast of a spot with a web address.

Nothing captures every lead, but these methods will help inform your marketing planning and decisions. Obviously, the bottom line is sales. So if a particular marketing mix is occurring and sales are happening… great! Even if you can't directly tie each lead to a specific marketing tactic, anecdotal feedback is valuable.

Don't fall prey to the siren's song of digital, either. A sales tactic of companies selling digital (whether email, search or display ads online, social media, even SEO) is that digital is preferable because it is trackable. That is true, but an effective marketing mix will invariably have digital and so-called traditional marketing tactics.

In tracking XYZ's lead sources, "Other" is defined as things that happen but not directly from a current marketing tactic. This could include leads that can't be tied directly to a tactic (even if we ask the prospect) or past prospects that suddenly reappear and inquire. It happens, so let's track it as best we can.

Based on data (or best guess), assign a number of leads delivered by each tactic. If the number is unknown, the lesson is to start to track the sources of leads. Remember, if no other method is available, ask the prospect how they heard about your company or offer.

For our example, the marketing tactics yield these results:
> **Website** - 500 inquiries via forms for more information or offers
> **Direct Mail** - response is 2% - returning a response card or calling for more information because of a mailing
> **Email** - response is 5% - clicking through from an email to the website
> **Word of Mouth** - 200 referrals
> **Other** - 100 leads

Note that the Direct Mail and Email responses mean returning a card asking for more information, calling. or clicking through and filling out a form from an email (this is one reason to use a purpose-built landing page with response form on the website which is used only for the email).

You may have multiple tactics that are "stacked" one after another - or are part of a multi-tactic campaign. It might include a mailing, email, and outbound phone call. This campaign model is much more powerful than a single tactic. Track the campaign results instead of the individual tactics. Example:
> **Spring Campaign** (mail, email, call) - 450 leads
> **Event Campaign** (pre-event contact, visit to booth, call) - 225 leads

For the XYZ example, we will stick with our simple numbers. Don't worry about having every number correct the first time through. The effort here is to put down your tactics, tag their effectiveness as best you can, make our calculations versus past performance then put it into practice. As you move forward, track the results of the different tactics and campaigns to determine a more informed estimate in the next planning cycle.

For the tactics that have a direct call to action and measurable response rate, in the example direct mail and email, we can calculate how much of each of those tactics we need in our plan to meet our sales goal. For those elements that don't have a response rate, such as website inquiries, we add the actual number of leads. Website, Word of Mouth, Advertising or other tactics can have a response or conversion rate. There are ways to improve response rate for all these tactics. For this exercise, simply use the actual numbers for planning.

For the response rate tactics, the number is calculated based on the amount of activity. If XYZ mailed 10,000 at 2% response, there are 200 leads; if 5,000 emails were sent, there are 250 resulting leads.

Let's look at how our past performance compares to meeting the goal for the next year:

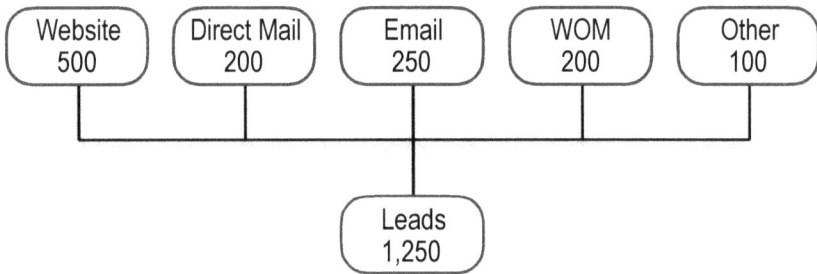

Website 500	Direct Mail 200	Email 250	WOM 200	Other 100

Leads 1,250

The 1,250 leads are added to the sales process and the numbers for each step calculated. Each step is affected by the lower than goal number of leads:

Step in Process	Goal	Projected
Leads	2000	1250
Meeting/Specs	1000	625
Estimate/Proposal	250	156
Close/Contract	50	31

This analysis shows that XYZ's level of marketing in the past year cannot meet the goal of the next year unless the rates of response are increased significantly.

If next year's results are the same as last year's performance, XYZ will close only 31 projects.

What's Next?
When the projection shows a shortfall versus goal, what is the next step? Perhaps the answer is as simple as increasing the number of direct mail pieces sent to suspects and prospects. Alternatively, a new tactic (for example,

Advertising) can be added to the marketing mix. However, there may be a way to increase the effectiveness of the current process.

In the XYZ example, an improvement in closing from five estimates per closed sale to three estimates per closed sale would result in 52 closed projects from the 1,250 leads currently expected. No additional marketing is needed at the top of the marketing process/funnel. It would be worth testing some ways of closing more estimates, perhaps making an extra follow up call to answer questions or adding some value to the deal.

Step in Process	Projected at 5/1	Projected at 3/1
Leads	1250	1250
Meeting/Specs	625	625
Estimate/Proposal	156	156
Close/Contract	31	52

The Bottom Line
The goal of this exercise is to begin to understand how to budget for marketing. Too often the amount of marketing done (and the tactics chosen) are not based on delivering the bottom line goal. The decisions are arbitrary or based on anecdote. This method of process analysis creates a good starting point. The model is refined each year based on new, real data.

Budgeting Time, Energy and Expertise
It is more challenging to create budgets for time, energy and expertise. Track the time that marketing planning and execution takes and assign a cost including salaries, benefits and a calculation of opportunity cost.

The purpose here is not to attempt to tie a dollar amount to each of these areas. More important to understand that when planning marketing, it is more than just budget dollars that are required.

Considering who (and how) staff will be involved in the marketing development and execution of tactics is critical to success. Let's look at an example of social media.

Social media is an excellent example of how much time, energy and expertise it takes to conduct marketing. Again, social media is "free". Posting to social media is easy. There is no cost to set up an account.

However, it takes quite a bit of effort to:
- Determine what should (and should not) be posted to social media,

- Develop content (text and photos),
- Create campaigns and contests,
- Build website pages to link social media to,
- Review/Approval of social media posts, and
- Communication internally of the planned posts and schedule (so staff can repost to their social media).

That looks like a list that takes time, energy and expertise. A company can outsource some parts of marketing (including social media), but it still requires internal resources to manage those external resources. Content heavy tactics (like social media) need internal time and energy to provide the information and reference material for external copywriters and content marketers.

Time

Often overlooked as a marketing resource is time. Time is sometimes used as an alternate to money. Meaning companies think of ways to use their staff time to reduce the cost of a project. That is fine… if a company can supply time to a project whether in planning, or producing, it does reduce cost. However, we often think we have more time than we do.

Time is also critical in ongoing communications strategies like email newsletters, PR or social media. I've talked to many companies who started a campaign but didn't allow for the time to continue producing the posts, emails or whatever. As a colleague of mine likes to say, "they go dark", not producing any new content. That's a problem. Usually, the media gets blamed, something like, "We tried social media, but didn't get anything out of it."

Expertise

Associated with time is the expertise of people. Many organizations have talented people who are interested in helping with marketing. They want to be involved. That is great! One of the planning steps for a project in the Genius Marketing process is putting together a roster of people who are involved in marketing (they aren't always from the Marketing Department – if there is one) who have the expertise (and time) to help build the plan, create the communications and manage the implementation.

This expertise within a company is critical for building the processes that sustain a communications campaign. Getting multiple people involved, using their gifts and interests to help promote the company can save external dollars paid for marketing expertise. It also helps build the fourth critical resource.

Energy

I sometimes call it "will". It's the capacity of an organization to get marketing done. It's great to consider the time and expertise internally we can commit to marketing, however, if we don't have the energy, it's better to consider buying services. Getting people involved can build energy. However, other factors in a company reduce energy.

For instance, if marketing tasks are added to already overwhelmed people's workload… energy will be low. Or, if an office move, new structure or other significant change is in the works, people won't have the energy to focus on marketing. They may want to be involved, but the other initiatives will reduce their will (or energy) on the marketing efforts.

Balance the Resources

So, it's not just about the money. All of the four elements must be considered as part of the resources a company brings to a marketing initiative. That's why Genius! Marketing helps companies build a plan that merges both available internal and external resources. It helps reduce cost and increases the success rate of marketing projects.

A good plan and mapping of processes result in the right mix of internal and external resources resulting in a "budget" for more than just financial considerations.

In the action planning chapter, there are tools for and instructions on how to organize the marketing team. These tools help visualize and communicate roles and responsibilities, and therefore, the time and expertise required of marketing team members.

The energy of an organization, you as an owner/manager, and of staff can be the hardest to determine. Realize that how busy people are in their standard work affects their energy for helping out with marketing. Some people will find working on marketing energizing. Others won't.

Marketing must happen throughout the year consistently. There are different times of year when more energy (and time) might be available. Develop marketing tactics and messages at those times. In the action planning chapter, there are scheduling tools to help plan the overall calendar and to consider when best to develop marketing.

CHAPTER 8
TAKEAWAYS AND EXERCISES

1. Budgeting for marketing can be process driven rather than arbitrary. Begin tracking the results of tactics and/or campaigns to determine the number of leads delivered.

2. Determine how much marketing is needed based on the sales or financial goals of the organization.

3. Consider the time, energy and expertise needed internally to manage and execute marketing properly. Consistently delivering your message and offer are more important than great creative. Don't let busyness or lack of resources to prevent consistent marketing.

4. Develop your need for marketing based on the goal and past performance. Track performance at each step in the process. Project the needed leads to reach your sales goal.

Performance	Step in Process	Goal
	1. Leads/Inquiries	
	2	
	3	
	4	
	5	
	6	
1 Sale	7. Closed Sale	

5. Track individual marketing tactics or campaigns to understand how many leads/inquiries each tactic or campaign delivers. New tactics can be tested, but track their results. The results of marketing must provide the leads needed to feed the sales process and meet the sales goal.

Website	DM	Email	WOM	Other

Leads

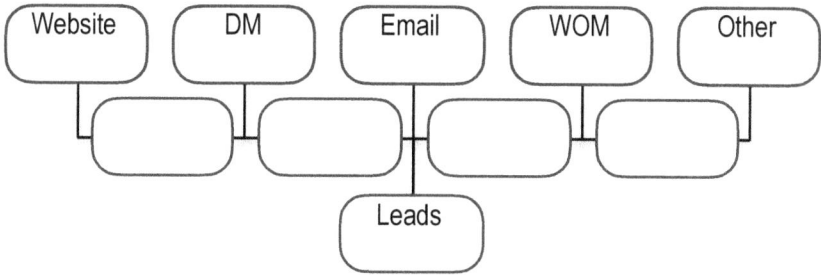

6. Use the tools in the action planning chapter to organize the marketing team and schedule.

9
ACTION PLANNING

"Plans are of little importance, but planning is essential."
— Winston Churchill

Genius! Marketing developed because of an interaction with a small business owner many years ago. Julie was a business owner who provided services to business-to-business customers. The company was Julie and a half-time employee. She asked me to review her company's marketing plan because she wasn't sure what to do next.

The plan was an impressive looking binder which on the cover had her company name and the logo of one of the boutique/hot agencies in our city. Julie told me she paid multiple thousand dollars for the plan. I reviewed the binder in an hour or so and took it back to Julie. I told her that she wasted her money.

The "marketing plan" was in the classic format of a formal business plan although being developed by an agency, it was incomplete. It covered the market, the brand and tactics anecdotally.

A formal, corporate marketing plan can include:
Executive Summary
Sales Strategy
Positioning
Pricing
Margin Structure
Discounts
Current Sales Process

Competitive/Industry Analysis
Marketing Responsibilities
Distribution Channels
Customer Service
Advertising and Promotion
Media Objectives and Strategy
Advertising Campaign
Promotion Strategy
Direct Sales
Communications/Literature
Suppliers
Public Relations
Publicity Strategy
PR
Editorial Strategy
Trade Shows
Internal Communications
Budget
Industry Averages
Anticipated Revenues
Measurements
Return on Investment
Implementation Schedule

The document associated with such a formal plan may be 25, 50 or 100 pages. It is entirely appropriate for a company with dedicated marketing staff and budget to purchase creative and media external resources.

The agency's plan for Julie didn't go into the depth of a full corporate formal plan. The tactics in Julie's plan ranged from a corporate brochure, direct mailer and other elements that the agency could provide (at additional cost) plus other tactics including PR, speaking and writing a book.

These weren't bad ideas. However, the plan cost Julie more than she had spent on marketing the previous year. Additionally, the plan did not consider how Julie would pay for, find the time for, or execute the tactics. How would she write a book? And set up speaking arrangements? And conduct a PR campaign in support of the book and speaking?

Julie thought she was getting a plan that would help her promote her company. What she got was a heavy burden.

Whether your organization includes you and an assistant, or one hundred employees, small businesses struggle with marketing because of the cost and the lack of time, energy and expertise to plan and execute marketing consistently.

My suggestion to Julie was to sit down with her and her assistant and decide on steps to help her move forward with her marketing. The result of our work together was an executable plan for her marketing and a new process. Initially called Marketing Coaching, because it focused on coaching a business owner or company manager through marketing processes, it grew into Genius! Marketing.

Question one in the process was this: If you could only do one thing to market/promote your company, what would it be?

This may seem overly simplistic, but it is at the crux of the Genius! Marketing system. It's not about which idea is most fabulous, but about the idea that will be effective and is executable with our budget and other resources! The plan can say to write a book, right up until Julie says "When will I have time to write a book!".

If you could only do one thing to promote your company, what would it be?

After determining what the top priority was for Julie's marketing, we chose second and third priorities. Could there be more than the 1, 2, 3 things? Yes, of course, but consider the typical To Do list. The more items on it, the harder it is to organize and get tasks done. Potential paralysis is overcome by prioritizing what must be done first. The simple plan uses this same methodology to make sure the most important and impactful tasks are accomplished.

A Simple Marketing Plan
For small businesses, a simple one-page marketing plan is sufficient. Other tools will be used to detail and organize the marketing activity. The advantage of the one-page plan is that it is simple, easy to remember and easy to communicate to internal and external resources. The Simple Plan could be for one division or product or service. Even with multiple plans, the one-page format keeps the efforts easy to communicate and organized. The Simple Plan has four sections.

1. **Offering** – what the company is marketing. This could be the entire

company offering or one specific product or service.

2. **Market** – the target audience.

3. **Marketing and Sales Activities** – it is essential to incorporate both marketing and sales to get a full picture of the effort.

4. **Accountability** – when and how the plan's effectiveness is evaluated.

The information in the simple plan will come from the work previously done in the Genius! Marketing process.

The Simple Marketing Plan

For XYZ Services Company

1. Our offerings are:
   Technical services; maintenance programs and safety training

2. Our market is:
   .1 All those who: *industrial companies that maintain their own equipment*
   .2 Included are those who: *use Chame, Bartone and Acme machining tools*
   .3 Major targets are: *companies within a 100-mile radius with $10M sales*

3. To exploit the market we shall:
   .1 *introduce our outsourced maintenance offering to 100 companies per year*
   .2 *educate prospects about the advantages and savings of outsourcing*
   .3 *offer a free machine inventory and maintenance checklist*
   .4 Provide Market Communications by: *flyers to support education events; website; digital including email, blog, news releases; and advertising in trade publications*
   .5 Select and train *two* sales personnel by: *August 31*
   .6 Assign markets, targets and goals for each by: *September 30*

4. Review results by *December 31* and modify elements accordingly by: *adding sales personnel, altering education delivery, adjusting advertising*

GeniusMarketing.com

Again, think of the Simple Plan as the mission statement of your marketing: designed to communicate the strategy of What (Offering), Who (Market/Audience) and How (Marketing and Sales ideas). It is the document that is used to give the big picture internally to the Marketing Committee/Team and externally to creative and production services. Review it at each monthly Marketing Meeting.

Once the Simple Plan is determined, move on to Action Planning. This is where the details of the "How" will be produced and executed.

Action Planning Tools

Action planning means getting into the details and moving beyond the idea to implementation or execution of the idea. There are several tools in the exercise section of this chapter which are templates for your organization to use.

Team Roles – determine who internally and externally will be part of your marketing team. This includes who will:

- Manage the processes,
- Come up with ideas,
- Evaluate the ideas and decide which to pursue,
- Develop the elements including content, design and production,
- Approve the elements,
- Implement or Execute the elements, and
- Evaluate the execution/effectiveness of the elements.

This could be a long list and include internal staff, agencies, digital marketers, webmasters, third-party suppliers of software (such as email marketing), and even marketing consultants like Genius! Marketing. It is crucial each team member understands their role and ultimately when and how they will be in the process of managing and implementing the marketing elements.

Distribution Schedule – decide delivery date of marketing elements. This is the overall calendar that your marketing team will manage to throughout the year. It will include dates of events, website updates, email sends, ad placements, and more. When reviewed monthly, it ensures that elements aren't forgotten, prepares the team for tasks to meet in the next month, quarter (and beyond), and opens any discussion needed about marketing elements that are overwhelming the team or budget.

It is also beneficial if a new product or service is coming to market during the coming year, to ensure that there are enough marketing elements scheduled to support the launch.

Editorial Calendar – in the age of content marketing, this calendar is critical; schedule when key messages will be communicated. As described in the message section of this book, the website is where all the information about your company, brand, and products resides. This calendar shows how you will communicate your messages over time… it schedules the conversations to have with prospects and customers over the course of the year. As shown in the sample calendar, every January is the opportunity to talk about "New Year's Resolutions" or "Things to Know - Trends for the New Year". Some messages that are seasonal… whether an industry event occurs once per year or a product or service is typically purchased during one time of the year.

This tool is critical in my consulting because it makes sure the organization is covering the topics that matter when they matter… and when there is the time in the schedule to communicate key value propositions and other messages that are not season-oriented. Not every prospect will see or hear every message but plan the schedule as if an ongoing conversation to support the sales process.

Element Control – manage the project. This tool shows who is doing what and the next steps in the production and distribution of the marketing element. It helps the manager manage, and the team develop and implement.

Week To Do – drills down to weekly tasks. For recurring elements (e.g., monthly email newsletter, social media, advertising), this sheet shows what needs to happen each week in the current month to ensure that elements are prepared and launched effectively.

The Process of Marketing

All of the tools in the Action Planning package are designed to avoid a common problem: the sudden realization that a marketing deadline is fast approaching and nothing has been developed to meet the deadline. It happens to organizations all the time, and the result is poor messaging, wasted money and inconsistent (or non-existent) marketing.

Genius! Marketing is designed to help alleviate this problem. By thinking about marketing and sales as a process, rather than an incongruous set of ideas and tactics, the organization can improve its marketing efficiency and effectiveness. The process focuses everyone involved with marketing and sales on the goal: getting more leads and ultimately, more sales.

CHAPTER 9
TAKEAWAYS AND EXERCISES

1. The best part of a one-page plan versus a fifty-page plan? These plans are actually implemented! People catch the vision, can keep the plan top-of-mind and act accordingly.

2. Action planning includes not only strategies and tactics but considers implementation – availability of resources, process changes, etc.

3. Hold a monthly Marketing Meeting – always have dates set to regroup, review and adjust the plan.

4. Questions for Creating the Plan
   What are our offerings?
   In particular, what are our offerings that are most needed or beneficial right now?

   _____
   _____
   _____

   Who is our market? _____
   On a gross level? Segmented by purchase type or other variables?

   _____
   _____
   _____

   What are the key segments that are best to target right now?

   _____
   _____
   _____

   What new or underserved markets can we target?

   _____
   _____
   _____

   How will we reach these markets?
     - What advantages do we have? How can we exploit them?
     - What are our messages? Media? Methods?
     - What new marketing communications do we need to reach our target segments?

   _____
   _____
   _____
   _____

Questions for Implementing the Plan
  - Who is going to do what?

_____
_____
_____

  - What resources do we have (time, energy, people, money)?

_____
_____
_____

  - How will we segment and test?

_____
_____
_____

What is success? What is our goal?

_____
_____
_____

  - When will we be done? Or at least regroup, check our results and change our plan?

_____
_____
_____

5. Use the other tools to organize and manage your marketing. Following are sample sheets and blank template.

The Simple Marketing Plan

For _____

1. Our offerings are: _____
    _____

2. Our market is:
    .1 _____

    .2 _____

    .3 _____

3. To exploit the market we shall:
    .1 _____

    .2 _____

    .3 _____

    .4 Provide Market Communications by: _____

    _____

    .5 Select and train _two_ sales personnel by: _____

    _____

    .6 Assign markets, targets and goals for each by: _____

4. Review results by _____ and modify elements accordingly by:

    _____

GeniusMarketing.com

Action Planning - Team Roster

SAMPLE

Name	Role	Current Marketing Touch Points	Potential Role/Touch Points
Bob	Manager, Sales	Direction, Content, Direct Sales	Newsletter editorials and other copy
Joe	Sales	Direct Sales, Networking	Coordinate database development
Sue	Sales, Technology	Direct Sales, Content	Content for e-mail and other materials
Sally	Inside Sales	Support	Up-sell/Cross-sell
Ralph	Production Manager, Customer Service	Support	?
Bill	Support		Follow-up, Fulfillment, Tracking
Intern	Support		Database development

Action Planning - Team Roster

Template

Name	Role	Current Marketing Touch Points	Potential Role/Touch Points

Action Planning - Marketing/Communications Schedule

SAMPLE

Tactic	January 1	2	3	4	February 1	2	3	4	March 1	2	3	4	April 1	2	3	4	May 1	2	3	4	June 1	2	3	4
Events			E																	E			E	
Advertising												Ad										Ad		
WOM																								
Blog		B						B				B		B						B			B	
Direct Mail														DM										
News Releases/Features																DM								
Email	EM				EM							EM		EM	EM			EM			EM			
Viral					V								V											V

Tactic	July 1	2	3	4	August 1	2	3	4	September 1	2	3	4	October 1	2	3	4	November 1	2	3	4	December 1	2	3	4
Events			E																	E			E	
Advertising												Ad										Ad		
WOM																								
Blog		B						B				B		B						B			B	
Direct Mail														DM										
News Releases/Features																DM								
Email	EM				EM							EM		EM	EM			EM			EM			
Viral					V								V											V

Action Planning - Marketing/Communications Schedule

Template

Tactic	January				February				March				April				May				June			
	1	2	3	4	1	2	3	4	1	2	3	4	1	2	3	4	1	2	3	4	1	2	3	4

Tactic	July				August				September				October				November				December			
	1	2	3	4	1	2	3	4	1	2	3	4	1	2	3	4	1	2	3	4	1	2	3	4

Marketing Element Themes/Editorial Schedule

SAMPLE

	January	February	March	April	May	June
	New Year Resolution	Product Launch	Benefit of DrySeal	Issues of Rain		
Website Update		x	x			
Blog	x	x	x	x		
News Releases						
Email	x	x	x	x		
Newsletter			x			
Viral/WOM	x	x				
Event				x		
Advertising		x				
Social Media	x					

	July	August	September	October	November	December
Website Update						
Blog						
News Releases						
Email						
Newsletter						
Viral/WOM						
Event						
Advertising						
Social Media						

Marketing Element Themes/Editorial Schedule

Template

January	February	March	April	May	June

July	August	September	October	November	December

SAMPLE

Element Responsibility and Tasks

Item	Responsible Person	Support Person(s)	Start Date	Distribution Date	Connected Tasks	Next Task
Brochure	Bob	Joe, Sue, Ralph	Current	Immediate	Review final	Go to print
E-mail	Joe	Sue, external	Current	1st week of month	Content schedule, get template designed	Get template in-house
Postcard	Sue	Ralph, Intern	Current	2nd week of month	Copy, design, print, set year schedule	Print current, content for v2
Web Update	Joe	Intern, external	?	?	?	Determine Schedule
Newsletter	Bob	Sue	Current	3rd week of month	Copy, design, print, set year schedule	Review design
Special Mailer	Bob			TBD	Copy, design, print	Determine Schedule (holiday, moving, other?)
Product Rollout	Joe	?	?	?	?	Determine what it is?
Leads/DB	Sue	Bob, Joe, Sally	Current	Ongoing	Clean out old contacts, Wayne to Chamber	Find North Hills suspects, Intern dial through contacts
News Release	Bob	External	Current	4th week of month	Copy, design, print, set schedule	Get PR guy the list of subjects
Event	Bob			TBD	Get speaker, location?	TBD
Case Histories	Bob	Sue	Current	Copy for 3 by 4/30	Design template	Collect customer stories
Message on Hold	Joe	External	Current	New scripts by 4/30	Production	Get writer script concepts

Element Responsibility and Tasks

Template

Item	Responsible Person	Support Person(s)	Start Date	Distriubtion Date	Connected Tasks	Next Task

Week by Week

SAMPLE

Item	First Week of Month	Second Week of Month	Third Week of Month	Fourth Week of Month
Brochure				
E-nail	Distribute	Determine content	Design/layout	Approval/distribution list check
Postcard	Approval/distribution list check	Distribute	Determine content	Design/layout
Web Update				
Newsletter	Design/layout	Approval/distribution list check	Distribute	Determine content
Special Mailer				
Web Portal				
Leads/DB	Add 25 new contacts	Add 25 new contacts	Add 25 new contacts	Add 25 new contacts
News Release		Determine content	Approval	Distribute
Event	As needed			
Case Histories	Review need quarterly			
Message on Hold	Review need quarterly			

Week by Week

Template

Item	First Week of Month	Second Week of Month	Third Week of Month	Fourth Week of Month

10
FINAL THOUGHTS AND NEXT STEPS

What is Genius?
That was the question asked at the beginning of this book. Perhaps when you opened this book, you thought it would be all about the next big idea. Clearly, ideas are needed, but ideas alone don't make genius… especially Genius! Marketing.

Now you know: genius isn't a scheme, it's a process. It is how an idea is implemented more than the idea itself. That's why this book focuses on the process of planning, the process of implementing, the process of managing the marketing.

This book was never intended to drill down into the management of individual ideas… such as "What's the best way to use email marketing?" There are many resources online featuring tips and tricks of particular tactics. From email to SEO to digital advertising… and so on. Read these tips and tricks. Learn the best practices. Just be sure you are integrating tactics into the marketing mix because you think the tactic will result in more sales. Check yourself not to "fall in love" with a tactic… because it's not about the idea, it's about the bottom line.

One resource for information about marketing tactics, best practices and tips/tricks is geniusmarketing.com, the "home" of Genius! Marketing.

Contact Genius! Marketing
If you have questions about the planning process or with best practices for individual tactics, contact me at eckert@geniusmarketing.com or visit the website. Sign up for our email newsletter or one of our webinars. Follow me @StephenLEckert on Twitter or LinkedIn.

Also available on the website are spreadsheet versions of the planning tools used throughout this book.

I'd be glad to help you through the planning process. I can meet with your team or facilitate the planning process remotely. Most planning projects can be accomplished in a few work sessions and move your organization quickly towards consistent implementation of marketing.

Virtual VP of Marketing

If more help is needed, I work with companies as a "Virtual Vice President of Marketing". I work with organizations that don't require a full-time marketing executive. The owner or CEO can no longer directly manage marketing effectively due to time constraints. The company doesn't have the internal staff with skills to manage the marketing either. This type of engagement can be for the short-term, as internal staff are prepared to manage the marketing, or as an ongoing engagement which saves an FTE.

Final Challenge

My challenge to you is to do the things that make marketing a success. If I had a 1, 2, 3 priority for you it would be this:

1. Go through the planning process. Do the work.

2. Hold a monthly marketing meeting… even if it is only with yourself.

3. Manage from the tools, especially the content and distribution calendars.

I believe any company can be a Genius! Marketing company. Here's hoping your organization becomes one.

May All Your Marketing Be Genius!,
SLEckert

CHAPTER 10
TAKEAWAYS

1. Contact me if you have questions about the Genius! Marketing process.

2. Follow me on Twitter or LinkedIn for updates and articles to help with your marketing.

3. If you need more help with planning or creating and managing tactics, contact me.

4. Do the work… be a genius!